Potluck Dishes

Jean Paré

companyscoming.com
visit our website

Front Cover

1. Sesame Seafood Bows, page 42
2. Strawberry Brownie Trifle, page 146
3. Pepper Beef Pinwheels, page 123
4. Thai Curry Chicken Wings, page 22

Props courtesy of:
Out of the Fire Studio
Strahl

Back Cover

1. Upside-Down Spread, page 15
2. Chili Cheese Bean Dip, page 11
3. Two Bean Dip, page 19

Props courtesy of:
Casa Bugatti
Island Pottery Inc.

We gratefully acknowledge the following suppliers for their generous support of our Test Kitchen and Photo Studio:

Broil King Barbecues®   Lagostina®
Corelle®   Proctor Silex® Canada
Hamilton Beach®   Tupperware®

Potluck Dishes

Second Printing August 2005

Library and Archives Canada Cataloguing in Publication
Paré, Jean, date
Company's Coming potluck dishes / Jean Paré.
(Original series)
Includes index.
ISBN 1-896891-81-0
1. Cookery. I. Title. II. Series.
TX731.P3715 2005   641.5   C2005-901599-3

Published by
Company's Coming Publishing Limited
2311 – 96 Street
Edmonton, Alberta T6N 1G3
Canada
Tel: 780-450-6223   Fax: 780-450-1857
www.companyscoming.com

Company's Coming is a registered trademark owned by
Company's Coming Publishing Limited

Printed in Canada

Need more recipes?

Six "***sneak preview***" recipes are featured online with every new book released.

Visit us at
www.companyscoming.com

Company's Coming Cookbooks

Original Series

- Softcover, 160 pages
- 6" x 9" (15 cm x 23 cm) format
- Lay-flat plastic comb binding
- Full-colour photos
- Nutrition information

Quick & easy recipes! Everyday ingredients!

Lifestyle Series

- Softcover, 160 pages
- 8" x 10" (20 cm x 25 cm) format
- Paperback
- Full-colour photos
- Nutrition information

Most Loved Recipe Collection

- Hardcover, 128 pages
- 8 3/4" x 8 3/4" (22 cm x 22 cm) format
- Durable sewn binding
- Full colour throughout
- Nutrition information

Special Occasion Series

- Hardcover & softcover, 192 pages
- 8 1/2" x 11" (22 cm x 28 cm) format
- Durable sewn binding
- Full colour throughout
- Nutrition information

See page 125 for more cookbooks.
For a complete listing, visit
www.companyscoming.com

Table of Contents

The Company's Coming Story 6

Foreword 7

Potluck Food Safety 8

Tips for Transporting Dishes 8

Planning a Potluck 9

Tips for the Potluck Guest 9

Appetizers 10

Breads & Quick Breads 26

Brunches 42

Casseroles 57

Main Dishes 68

Salads 91

Side Dishes 102

Soups & Sandwiches 114

Desserts 128

Measurement Tables 150

Recipe Index 151

Mail Order Form 158

What's New! 159

Cookbook Checklist 160

Foreword

Appetizers

Brunches

Casseroles

Salads

Desserts

Recipe Index

What's New!

The Company's Coming Story

Jean Paré (pronounced "Perry") grew up understanding that the combination of family, friends and home cooking is the best recipe for a good life. From her mother, she learned to appreciate good cooking, while her father praised even her earliest attempts in the kitchen. When Jean left home, she took with her many acquired family recipes, a love of cooking and an intriguing desire to read recipe books like novels!

"never share a recipe you wouldn't use yourself"

In 1963, when her four children had all reached school age, Jean volunteered to cater the 50th Anniversary of the Vermilion School of Agriculture, now Lakeland College, in Alberta, Canada. Working out of her home, Jean prepared a dinner for over 1,000 people which launched a flourishing catering operation that continued for over eighteen years. During that time, she was provided with countless opportunities to test new ideas with immediate feedback—resulting in empty plates and contented customers! Whether preparing cocktail sandwiches for a house party or serving a hot meal for 1,500 people, Jean Paré earned a reputation for good food, courteous service and reasonable prices.

As requests for her recipes mounted, Jean was often asked the question, "Why don't you write a cookbook?" Jean responded by teaming up with her son, Grant Lovig, in the fall of 1980 to form Company's Coming Publishing Limited. The publication of the first Company's Coming cookbook on April 14, 1981 marked the debut of what would soon become one of the world's most popular cookbook series.

The company has grown since those early days when Jean worked from a spare bedroom in her home. Today she leads a team of writers and testers in the development of new recipes. Under the guidance of Jean's daughter, Gail Lovig, Company's Coming cookbooks are now distributed throughout Canada, in addition to the United States and numerous overseas markets. Rounding off three generations is Jean's granddaughter (Grant's daughter), Amanda Jean Lovig, who looks after publicity and arranges personal appearances for her grandmother.

Bestsellers many times over in English, Company's Coming cookbooks have also been published in French and Spanish. Familiar and trusted in home kitchens around the world, Company's Coming cookbooks are offered in a variety of formats. Highly regarded as kitchen workbooks, the softcover Original Series, with its lay-flat plastic comb binding, is still the favourite with readers.

Jean Paré's approach to cooking has always called for *quick and easy recipes* using *everyday ingredients.* Even when travelling, she is constantly on the lookout for new ideas to share with her readers. At home, she can usually be found researching and writing recipes, or helping in the company's test kitchen. Jean continues to gain new supporters by adhering to what she calls The Golden Rule of Cooking: *"Never share a recipe you wouldn't use yourself."* It's an approach that has worked—*millions of times over!*

Foreword

Potluck—an intriguing combination of food and luck, where guests share whatever they happen to bring. It's an old-fashioned idea that sounds great until everyone arrives with a pan of brownies and there's a hungry crowd to feed! When I was part of such an event, "eat dessert first" took on a whole new meaning and *Potluck Dishes* was born. A little planning goes a long way to creating the perfect potluck, and this book will help you do just that.

Whether you're the host of the event or an invited guest, *Potluck Dishes* puts everything you need at your fingertips, including pointers for planning a well-rounded meal, setting up the buffet, choosing the perfect dish, and safely transporting your dish to your destination. We also offer food safety guidelines, helping you to ensure a healthy event for all, and Potluck Suggestions indicating just how far a dish will stretch when you're one of many bringing a particular course.

There's a smorgasbord of crowd-pleasing salads, side dishes, main dishes and desserts in *Potluck Dishes*, and a feast of colourful pictures that show you how to plan a potluck with an inviting and delicious theme. With ten Company's Coming Classic recipes—including such hits as Japanese Cabbage Salad, Surprise Spread, and Oriental Wings—your contribution to any potluck is sure to get rave reviews.

Church congregations, sports leagues, block parties, gatherings with colleagues and friends—groups of all types and sizes love to socialize and share great food. No matter what the occasion, whenever a hungry group gets together, potluck is the answer—a fun, easy way to entertain a few or feed a crowd, especially for today's busy cooks. Everyone makes a little, everyone enjoys a lot, and no one spends all day in the kitchen.

With a little planning and a little help from *Potluck Dishes*, everyone will enjoy a delicious meal—and eating dessert first will be by choice rather than by chance.

Jean Paré

Nutrition Information Guidelines

Each recipe is analyzed using the most current version of the Canadian Nutrient File from Health Canada, which is based on the United States Department of Agriculture (USDA) Nutrient Database.

- If more than one ingredient is listed (such as "hard margarine or butter"), or if a range is given (1 – 2 tsp., 5 – 10 mL), only the first ingredient or first amount is analyzed.

- For meat, poultry and fish, the serving size per person is based on the recommended 4 oz. (113 g) uncooked weight (without bone), which is 2 – 3 oz. (57 – 85 g) cooked weight (without bone)—approximately the size of a deck of playing cards.

- Milk used is 1% M.F. (milk fat), unless otherwise stated.

- Cooking oil used is canola oil, unless otherwise stated.

- Ingredients indicating "sprinkle," "optional," or "for garnish" are not included in the nutrition information.

Margaret Ng, B.Sc. (Hon.), M.A.
Registered Dietitian

Potluck Food Safety

Maintaining safe food temperatures and a healthy food environment is critical potluck practice. To prevent the growth of harmful bacteria that leads to food spoilage, follow these helpful guidelines:

- Cook foods completely before taking them to the potluck. Never transport partially cooked foods and finish cooking them at your destination.

- Hot foods must be kept piping hot 165°F (73°C) or hotter. As guests arrive, put hot foods in the oven. Use chafing dishes and portable cooking fuel, slow cookers or warming trays to keep foods hot at serving time.

- As guests arrive, put cold foods in the refrigerator. Cold foods must be kept at 40°F (4°C) or colder, especially items containing eggs, dairy products or seafood.

- Follow the 2 hour rule: never allow food to linger on a buffet table for more than 2 hours. Set out smaller portions and be sure to use clean serving dishes when refilling.

- Reserve portions of temperature-sensitive foods in the oven or refrigerator for guests who will be arriving late.

- Place spoons in dips and sauces to prevent double-dipping.

Tips for Transporting Dishes

- If you don't have an insulated container to transport hot dishes, wrap them in foil and then with heavy towels or layers of newspaper.

- To keep a casserole lid in place during transport, wrap a thick rubber band around the casserole handle and criss-cross around the lid handle. Repeat with the opposite casserole handle.

- To keep stovetop foods hot, transfer them to a warmed casserole. Cover. Wrap the casserole with heavy towels or put it into an insulated or quilted pouch designed for transporting hot foods.

- Pack cold foods, especially those made with eggs, dairy products or mayonnaise, in a cooler with ice or frozen gel packs to keep at safe temperatures during transport.

- To be sure that your salad is crisp at a potluck, pack the dressing, garnishes and greens in separate containers. Assemble and toss your salad just before serving.

- To keep open-face sandwiches looking nice when transporting, arrange in a single layer in an airtight container with enough headspace so that filling and garnishes are not flattened.

- Hot soup may be transported in the pot or transferred to a slow cooker. Place in a heavy cardboard box and steady with towels. For added stability, set the box on the floor of your vehicle, rather than on the seat. Be sure to take along an extension cord in case you need one for the slow cooker.

Planning a Potluck

Originally, potlucks were spontaneous gatherings. Everyone brought whatever they chose to prepare. A planned potluck, where the various elements are assigned, offers a wide variety of dishes and ensures delicious results.

- When planning a full course potluck, assign guests a specific element of the meal, such as an appetizer, salad, main course or dessert. Assign beverages, buns or pickles to people who don't cook or who have a longer distance to travel.

- Try planning a potluck around a theme, such as an Italian or Mexican potluck. Or have a salad potluck for lunch with a small group, or a dessert potluck for an evening with friends. Have each guest bring an appropriate dish to suit the event. You'll find ideas for various kinds of potlucks in the photo legends throughout this book.

- Both spontaneous and planned, potlucks are great for larger groups. You can prevent congestion and encourage guests to mingle by planning separate serving areas for beverages and desserts. Alternatively, organize a single table with plates, napkins and cutlery at one end; appetizers, salads and buns to start; main courses in the middle; and desserts, beverages and glasses at the opposite end.

- For a smaller potluck, you can provide the main course, with your guests supplying the side dishes and dessert.

Tips for the Potluck Guest

Potluck dinners are wonderful opportunities to get together with family and friends and share a favourite recipe. Keep the following tips in mind when planning your contribution:

- When you are one of many people contributing, your item doesn't need to serve the entire guest list. A good rule of thumb is to bring a dish that will serve your own family plus a few extra people. If you are responsible for providing an entire course, ask the host how many people are expected and plan accordingly.

- Whenever possible, bring a ready-to-eat dish. Remember that your host's refrigerator, oven or counter space may be limited. If items need to be sliced or cut, do so before taking them to the potluck.

- Before bringing soup, check with the host to ensure that soup spoons and bowls will be available. If you're planning to take soup in a pot, ask your host if a stovetop burner will be available. Alternatively, you will need an electrical outlet for a slow cooker to keep soup piping hot.

- Remember to bring serving utensils appropriate for your dish. Label your utensils, serving dishes or appliances with your name to ensure they are returned to you.

Crisp Fried Wontons

Serve with sweet and sour sauce or plum sauce for dipping.
Make these ahead and freeze (see Tip, page 23).

CHICKEN FILLING

Large egg	1	1
Soy sauce	1 1/2 tbsp.	25 mL
Salt	1/4 tsp.	1 mL
Ground chicken	3/4 lb.	340 g
Finely chopped bamboo shoots or water chestnuts)	1/4 cup	60 mL
Chopped green onion	1/4 cup	60 mL
Water	1 tsp.	5 mL
Cornstarch	1 tsp.	5 mL
Package of wonton wrappers	16 oz.	454 g
Milk	1/4 cup	60 mL

Cooking oil, for deep-frying

Chicken Filling: Beat egg, soy sauce and salt with fork in medium bowl.

Add ground chicken, bamboo shoots and onion. Mix well.

Stir water into cornstarch in small cup until smooth. Add to chicken mixture. Mix well. Makes about 2 cups (500 mL) filling.

Work with wonton wrappers 1 at a time. Keep remaining wrappers covered with damp tea towel to prevent drying. Place 1 wrapper diagonally on work surface. Spoon about 1 tsp. (5 mL) filling onto centre of wrapper. Dampen edges of wrapper with milk. Fold bottom corner up and over filling, aligning with top corner to form triangle. Press edges together to seal. Dampen side corners with milk. Bring up side corners and pinch together over filling. Cover with damp tea towel. Repeat with remaining wrappers, filling and milk.

Deep-fry wontons in small batches in hot (375°F, 190°C) cooking oil for about 2 minutes per batch until crisp and golden. Remove with slotted spoon to paper towels to drain. Makes about 90 wontons.

1 wonton: 44 Calories; 3 g Total Fat (1.4 g Mono, 0.7 g Poly, 0.2 g Sat); 3 mg Cholesterol; 3 g Carbohydrate; trace Fibre; 1 g Protein; 56 mg Sodium

Appetizers

Chili Cheese Bean Dip

A sourdough bread bowl holds a peppery cheese dip. You can vary the heat by your choice of salsa. Add vegetable sticks or crackers to the plate, along with the bread cubes, for dipping.

Can of romano beans, rinsed and drained	19 oz.	540 mL
Salsa	1 cup	250 mL
Diced pasteurized cheese loaf (such as Velveeta)	3/4 cup	175 mL
Block of cream cheese, softened and cut up	4 oz.	125 g
Diced green pepper	1/4 cup	60 mL
Sliced green onion	1/4 cup	60 mL
Chili powder	2 tsp.	10 mL
Garlic clove, minced (or 1/4 tsp., 1 mL, powder), optional	1	1
Dried crushed chilies	1/4 tsp.	1 mL
Sourdough bread loaf (about 8 inch, 20 cm, diameter)	1	1
Chopped fresh cilantro or parsley (optional)	2 tsp.	10 mL

Coarsely mash beans with fork in large bowl.

Add next 8 ingredients. Stir well.

Cut 1/2 to 3/4 inch (1.2 to 2 cm) from top of bread loaf. Set aside top. Remove bread from inside of loaf, leaving about 3/4 inch (2 cm) thick shell. Set aside removed bread. Spoon cheese mixture into hollowed loaf. Replace top. Wrap loaf with foil. Bake in 300°F (150°C) oven for about 2 hours until heated through and cheese is melted. Remove from oven. Discard foil. Remove loaf to large serving plate. Remove top of loaf. Break up and use for dipping.

Sprinkle cilantro over cheese mixture. Cut reserved bread into bite-size pieces for dipping. Arrange around loaf. Serves 10.

1 serving: 268 Calories; 10.3 g Total Fat (3.1 g Mono, 0.7 g Poly, 5.7 g Sat); 25 mg Cholesterol; 34 g Carbohydrate; 4 g Fibre; 11 g Protein; 778 mg Sodium

Pictured on page 18 and on back cover.

California Rolls

These colourful appetizers take a bit of time to prepare, but are well worth the effort. They'll get rave reviews at any potluck!

SUSHI RICE		
Short grain white rice	1 1/2 cups	375 mL
Cold water		
Water	2 cups	500 mL
Rice (or white wine) vinegar	3 tbsp.	50 mL
Mirin (Japanese sweet cooking seasoning), or medium sherry	3 tbsp.	50 mL
Granulated sugar	2 tbsp.	30 mL
Salt	1 tsp.	5 mL
Cooking oil	1 tsp.	5 mL
Large egg, fork-beaten	1	1
Nori (roasted seaweed) sheets	4	4
Mayonnaise (not salad dressing)	1/4 cup	60 mL
Wasabi paste (Japanese horseradish)	2 tsp.	10 mL
English cucumber (with peel), cut into 3 inch (7.5 cm) long slivers	1/4	1/4
Ripe small avocado, cut into slivers	1/2	1/2
Imitation crabmeat (or crabmeat, drained and cartilage removed), flaked	3 1/2 oz.	100 g
Red medium pepper, seeds and ribs removed, cut into long slivers	1/4	1/4
Grated carrot	2 tbsp.	30 mL
Water		
Tamari (or soy sauce), for dipping		

Sushi Rice: Rinse rice with cold water several times until water is no longer cloudy. Drain. Put into medium bowl. Add cold water until rice is covered. Let stand for 30 minutes. Drain. Transfer to medium saucepan.

Add second amount of water. Bring to a boil on high. Reduce heat to low. Cover. Simmer for 20 minutes, without stirring. Remove from heat. Let stand for 10 minutes.

(continued on next page)

Appetizers

Combine next 4 ingredients in small bowl. Add to rice. Stir. Cool. Makes about 4 cups (1 L) sushi rice.

Heat cooking oil in small frying pan on low. Add egg. Cook without turning, until egg is set. Transfer to cutting board. Cut egg into thin strips.

Place 1 nori sheet, shiny-side down, on small bamboo mat or heavy cloth napkin. With wet fork, spread about 1 cup (250 mL) sushi rice on nori, leaving about 2 inch (5 cm) edge on long side furthest from you (see diagram 1).

Combine mayonnaise and wasabi paste in small cup. Spread 1 tbsp. (15 mL) wasabi mixture in a narrow strip on rice, 1 inch (2 cm) from edge closest to you (see diagram 2). Layer 1/4 of egg strips on top of wasabi mixture.

Layer 1/4 each of next 5 ingredients, in order given, on top of egg strips.

Dampen uncovered edge of nori with water. Bring long edge closest to you up and over vegetables to enclose (see diagram 3). Using mat, roll nori back and forth to pack filling and vegetables tightly. Seal roll by rolling onto uncovered edge of nori. Repeat with remaining nori sheets, filling, wasabi mixture, egg strips and vegetables. Wrap each roll with plastic wrap. Chill for at least 1 hour. Discard plastic wrap. Trim ends. Cut each roll into 6 equal slices. Serve with tamari. Makes 24 slices.

1 slice: 88 Calories; 3.1 g Total Fat (1.7 g Mono, 0.8 g Poly, 0.4 g Sat); 11 mg Cholesterol; 13 g Carbohydrate; trace Fibre; 2 g Protein; 151 mg Sodium

Pictured on page 17.

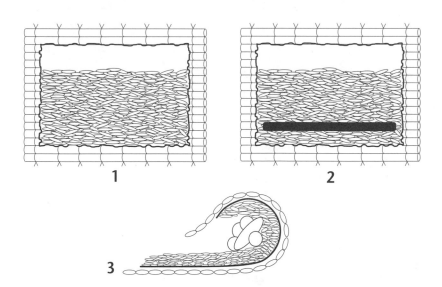

1

2

3

Ginger Pork Spring Rolls

*A crispy, tasty finger food. Serve with plum sauce or Indonesian
sweet soy sauce for dipping. Make these ahead and freeze (see Tip, page 23).*

GINGER PORK FILLING

Lean ground pork	6 oz.	170 g
Grated carrot	1/4 cup	60 mL
Thinly sliced green onion	2 tbsp.	30 mL
Indonesian sweet (or thick) soy sauce	1 1/2 tbsp.	25 mL
Cornstarch	2 tsp.	10 mL
Sesame oil, for flavour	1 tsp.	5 mL
Garlic clove, minced (or 1/4 tsp., 1 mL, powder)	1	1
Finely grated, peeled gingerroot (or 1/8 tsp., 0.5 mL, ground ginger)	1/2 tsp.	2 mL
Water	2 tbsp.	30 mL
All-purpose flour	2 tbsp.	30 mL
Spring roll wrappers (6 inch, 15 cm, square)	18	18

Cooking oil, for deep-frying

Ginger Pork Filling: Combine first 8 ingredients in medium bowl. Makes about 1 1/4 cups (300 mL) filling.

Stir water into flour in small cup until smooth.

Work with spring roll wrappers 1 at a time. Keep remaining wrappers covered with damp tea towel to prevent drying. Place 1 wrapper diagonally on work surface. Spoon about 1 tbsp. (15 mL) filling onto wrapper near bottom corner. Dampen edges of wrapper with flour mixture. Fold bottom corner over filling. Fold side corners over filling. Roll up tightly toward top corner to seal. Cover with damp tea towel. Repeat with remaining wrappers, filling and flour mixture.

Deep-fry spring rolls in 2 or 3 batches in hot (375°F, 190°C) cooking oil for about 2 minutes per batch until pork is no longer pink and wrapper is golden. Remove with slotted spoon to paper towels to drain. Makes 18 spring rolls.

(continued on next page)

Appetizers

1 spring roll: 162 Calories; 6.7 g Total Fat (3.5 g Mono, 1.8 g Poly, 1 g Sat); 9 mg Cholesterol; 20 g Carbohydrate; trace Fibre; 5 g Protein; 271 mg Sodium

Pictured on page 17.

Upside-Down Spread

Smooth cream cheese mellows layers of tangy tomato, basil and pecans.
Surround this unique appetizer with an assortment of crackers.
Looks great on a holiday potluck table.

Sun-dried tomatoes in oil, drained and chopped	1 cup	250 mL
Chopped pecans, toasted (see Tip, page 22)	1 cup	250 mL
Basil pesto	1/2 cup	125 mL
Blocks of cream cheese (8 oz., 250 g, each), softened	3	3
Fresh basil leaves, for garnish	4	4

Combine sun-dried tomato, pecans and pesto in medium bowl.

Line inside of separate medium bowl with plastic wrap. Spread 1 block of cream cheese evenly in bottom of bowl. Spread 1/2 of sun-dried tomato mixture on top of cream cheese to side of bowl. Continue layering, spreading second block of cream cheese, remaining sun-dried tomato mixture and third block of cream cheese, in order given, to side of bowl. Cover. Chill for about 3 hours until firm. Gently loosen plastic wrap around bowl. Invert cheese spread onto large serving plate. Discard plastic wrap.

Garnish with basil leaves. Makes about 5 cups (1.25 L).

2 tbsp. (30 mL): 96 Calories; 9.6 g Total Fat (3.9 g Mono, 0.9 g Poly, 4.3 g Sat); 20 mg Cholesterol; 2 g Carbohydrate; trace Fibre; 2 g Protein; 61 mg Sodium

Pictured on page 18 and on back cover.

Oriental Wings

First published in Appetizers, *these first-rate chicken wings marinate as they cook. A perfect potluck appetizer that's easy to prepare.*

Whole chicken wings, split in half and tips discarded (or chicken drumettes)	3 lbs.	1.4 kg
Soy sauce	1 cup	250 mL
Granulated sugar	1/2 cup	125 mL
Water	1/2 cup	125 mL
Salt	1/2 tsp.	2 mL
Ground ginger	1/4 tsp.	1 mL
Garlic powder	1/4 tsp.	1 mL

Arrange wing pieces in single layer in ungreased 3 quart (3 L) shallow baking dish or large roasting pan.

Combine remaining 6 ingredients in small bowl. Pour over wing pieces. Bake, uncovered, in 350°F (175°C) oven for 1 1/2 to 2 hours, turning wing pieces at halftime, until tender. Makes about 36 wing pieces (or 24 drumettes).

1 wing piece: 62 Calories; 3.3 g Total Fat (1.3 g Mono, 0.7 g Poly, 0.9 g Sat); 16 mg Cholesterol; 4 g Carbohydrate; 0 g Fibre; 4 g Protein; 531 mg Sodium

Variation: Omit sugar. Use same amount of liquid honey.

Asian Potluck
1. California Rolls, page 12
2. Thai Slaw, page 95
3. Sweet And Sour Pork, page 86
4. Ginger Pork Spring Rolls, page 14

Props courtesy of: Cherison Enterprises Inc.
Island Pottery Inc.

Appetizers

Two Bean Dip

Two bean, or not two bean? No need to question this one—it's a winner!
Serve with vegetable crackers or pita chips for a casual
gathering or southwestern potluck.

Can of chickpeas (garbanzo beans), rinsed and drained	19 oz.	540 mL
Can of white kidney beans, rinsed and drained	19 oz.	540 mL
Lemon juice	1/2 cup	125 mL
Olive oil	1 tbsp.	15 mL
Garlic cloves, minced (or 3/4 tsp., 4 mL, powder)	3	3
Drops of hot pepper sauce	4	4
Salt	1/2 tsp.	2 mL
Chopped fresh parsley (or 3/4 tsp., 4 mL, flakes)	1 tbsp.	15 mL

Combine first 7 ingredients in large bowl. Process in 2 batches in blender or food processor, scraping down sides if necessary, until smooth. Transfer to medium bowl.

Add parsley. Stir well. Makes about 3 1/2 cups (875 mL).

2 tbsp. (30 mL): 30 Calories; 0.7 g Total Fat (0.4 g Mono, 0.2 g Poly, 0.1 g Sat); 0 mg Cholesterol; 5 g Carbohydrate; 1 g Fibre; 2 g Protein; 86 mg Sodium

Pictured on page 18 and on back cover.

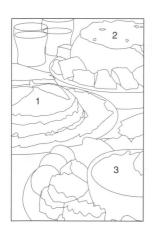

Dips
1. Upside-Down Spread, page 15
2. Chili Cheese Bean Dip, page 11
3. Two Bean Dip, above

Props courtesy of: Casa Bugatti
                       Island Pottery Inc.

Eggplant Onion Dip

A unique dip to serve with pita bread chips or vegetables. The mildly spiced flavour will have everyone returning for more.

Medium eggplants	3	3
Olive (or cooking) oil	3 tbsp.	50 mL
Chopped onion	1 1/2 cups	375 mL
Garlic cloves, minced (or 3/4 tsp., 4 mL, powder)	3	3
Salt	1 tsp.	5 mL
Ground cumin	1/4 tsp.	1 mL
Ground coriander	1/4 tsp.	1 mL
Cayenne pepper	1/8 tsp.	0.5 mL
Chopped fresh parsley	3 tbsp.	50 mL
Tahini (sesame paste)	2 tbsp.	30 mL
Lemon juice	2 tbsp.	30 mL

With fork, randomly poke several holes into each eggplant. Place on foil-lined baking sheet. Bake in 450°F (230°C) oven for about 45 minutes until softened. Let stand for about 10 minutes until cool enough to handle. Cut each eggplant in half lengthwise. Discard seeds. Scoop out flesh into food processor. Discard shells. Pulse with on/off motion until finely chopped. Transfer to medium bowl.

Heat olive oil in large frying pan on medium. Add onion and garlic. Cook for 10 to 15 minutes, stirring often, until onion is caramelized.

Add next 4 ingredients. Heat and stir on medium-low for about 5 minutes until fragrant. Add to eggplant. Stir well.

Add parsley, tahini and lemon juice. Stir well. Chill for 1 hour. Makes about 2 1/2 cups (625 mL).

2 tbsp. (30 mL): 44 Calories; 2.4 g Total Fat (1.6 g Mono, 0.3 g Poly, 0.3 g Sat); 0 mg Cholesterol; 6 g Carbohydrate; 2 g Fibre; 1 g Protein; 117 mg Sodium

Pictured on page 89.

Layered Tex-Mex Dip

Kids and adults will enjoy this creamy dip with a subtle chili heat. Serve with lots of tortilla chips or vegetable sticks at a Mexican potluck.

Cooking oil	1 tsp.	5 mL
Lean ground beef	1 lb.	454 g
Finely chopped onion	1 cup	250 mL
Ketchup	1/2 cup	125 mL
Chili powder	1 tsp.	5 mL
Granulated sugar	1/2 tsp.	2 mL
Salt	1/2 tsp.	2 mL
Pepper	1/4 tsp.	1 mL
Block of light cream cheese, softened	8 oz.	250 g
Light sour cream	1 cup	250 mL
Can of diced green chilies, drained	4 oz.	113 g
Thinly sliced green onion	1/4 cup	60 mL
Grated light sharp Cheddar cheese	1 1/4 cups	300 mL
Chili powder	1/4 tsp.	1 mL

Heat cooking oil in large frying pan on medium. Add ground beef and onion. Scramble-fry for 5 to 10 minutes until beef is no longer pink. Drain.

Add next 5 ingredients. Stir well. Remove from heat. Cool.

Beat cream cheese and sour cream in medium bowl until smooth. Spread evenly in bottom of greased 9 inch (22 cm) pie plate. Spread beef mixture on top.

Sprinkle chilies, green onion and Cheddar cheese, in order given, over beef mixture.

Sprinkle second amount of chili powder over Cheddar cheese. Bake in 400°F (205°C) oven for about 15 minutes until heated through and cheese is bubbling. Makes about 4 cups (1 L).

2 tbsp. (30 mL): 66 Calories; 4.2 g Total Fat (1.6 g Mono, 0.2 g Poly, 2.5 g Sat); 16 mg Cholesterol; 2 g Carbohydrate; trace Fibre; 5 g Protein; 191 mg Sodium

Thai Curry Chicken Wings

Slightly sweet with a mild heat.
Tasty Thai flavours make a scrumptious treat!

CURRY MARINADE

Salted peanuts	1/2 cup	125 mL
Sweet chili sauce	1/2 cup	125 mL
Lime juice	1/4 cup	60 mL
Fresh cilantro or parsley, lightly packed	1/4 cup	60 mL
Red curry paste	1 tbsp.	15 mL
Garlic cloves, minced (or 1/2 tsp., 2 mL, powder)	2	2
Finely grated, peeled gingerroot (or 1/4 tsp., 1 mL, ground ginger)	1 tsp.	5 mL
Whole chicken wings, split in half and tips discarded (or chicken drumettes)	3 lbs.	1.4 kg

Curry Marinade: Process first 7 ingredients in blender or food processor until smooth. Makes about 1 cup (250 mL) marinade.

Put wing pieces into large resealable freezer bag. Pour marinade over top. Seal bag. Turn until coated. Marinate in refrigerator for at least 6 hours or overnight, turning occasionally. Discard marinade. Arrange wing pieces in single layer on greased wire racks set in 2 foil-lined baking sheets with sides. Bake in 350°F (175°C) oven for about 1 hour, switching position of baking sheets at halftime, until wing pieces are tender. Makes about 36 wing pieces (or 24 drumettes).

1 wing piece: 76 Calories; 5.1 g Total Fat (2.1 g Mono, 1.2 g Poly, 1.2 g Sat); 17 mg Cholesterol; 2 g Carbohydrate; trace Fibre; 6 g Protein; 88 mg Sodium

Pictured on front cover.

 To toast nuts, seeds or coconut, spread evenly in ungreased shallow pan. Bake in 350°F (175°C) oven for 5 to 10 minutes, stirring or shaking often, until desired doneness.

Appetizers

Polynesian Meatballs

These succulent meatballs first appeared in Appetizers *and are a tried-and-true hit! Take the sweet and sour apricot-flavoured sauce in a separate container to serve on the side.*

Can of water chestnuts, drained and finely chopped	8 oz.	227 mL
Soy sauce	3 tbsp.	50 mL
Brown sugar, packed (or granulated sugar)	1 tbsp.	15 mL
Garlic cloves, minced (or 1/2 tsp., 2 mL, powder)	2	2
Parsley flakes	1 tsp.	5 mL
Onion powder	1/2 tsp.	2 mL
Lean ground beef	2 lbs.	900 g
APRICOT SAUCE		
Apricot jam	1 cup	250 mL
Apple cider vinegar	3 tbsp.	50 mL
Paprika	1/4 tsp.	1 mL

Combine first 6 ingredients in large bowl.

Add ground beef. Mix well. Roll into 1 inch (2.5 cm) balls. Arrange in single layer in ungreased baking sheet with sides. Bake in 375°F (190°C) oven for about 15 minutes until meatballs are no longer pink inside. Makes about 6 1/2 dozen (78) meatballs.

Apricot Sauce: Combine jam, vinegar and paprika in small bowl. Makes about 1 cup (250 mL) sauce. Serve with meatballs. Serves 8.

1 serving: 371 Calories; 17.1 g Total Fat (7.4 g Mono, 0.7 g Poly, 6.8 g Sat); 63 mg Cholesterol; 33 g Carbohydrate; trace Fibre; 22 g Protein; 486 mg Sodium

Potluck Suggestion: Serves up to 20.

To freeze deep-fried appetizers, arrange in a single layer on a waxed paper-lined baking sheet and freeze. Store frozen pieces in an airtight container in the freezer. To reheat, arrange pieces in a single layer on an ungreased baking sheet. Bake in a 350°F (175°C) oven for about 15 minutes until heated through.

Mini Oriental Spring Rolls

These bite-size, mildly spiced appetizers are appealing on a potluck table and are just right for dipping. Make these ahead and freeze (see Tip, page 23).

ORIENTAL CHICKEN FILLING

Cooking oil	1 tbsp.	15 mL
Boneless, skinless chicken breast half, cut julienne (see Note)	4 oz.	113 g
Grated carrot	1/4 cup	60 mL
Shredded suey choy (Chinese cabbage), or green cabbage	1/4 cup	60 mL
Chopped fresh bean sprouts	1 cup	250 mL
Green onions, thinly sliced	3	3
Granulated sugar	1/2 tsp.	2 mL
Salt	1/2 tsp.	2 mL
Garlic powder	1/8 tsp.	0.5 mL
Soy sauce	2 tsp.	10 mL
Wonton wrappers	38	38
Water		

Cooking oil, for deep-frying

Oriental Chicken Filling: Heat wok or large frying pan on medium-high until very hot. Add first amount of cooking oil. Add chicken, carrot and suey choy. Stir-fry for about 1 minute until chicken is no longer pink. Reduce heat to medium.

Add next 5 ingredients. Stir-fry for 2 minutes.

Add soy sauce. Stir-fry for about 2 minutes until liquid is evaporated. Cool. Drain. Chop chicken mixture. Makes about 1 cup (250 mL) filling.

Work with wonton wrappers 1 at a time. Keep remaining wrappers covered with damp tea towel to prevent drying. Place 1 wrapper diagonally on work surface. Spoon about 1 tsp. (5 mL) filling onto wrapper near bottom corner. Dampen edges of wrapper with water. Fold bottom corner over filling. Fold side corners over filling. Roll up tightly toward top corner to seal. Cover with damp tea towel. Repeat with remaining wrappers, filling and water.

(continued on next page)

Deep-fry spring rolls in 5 or 6 batches in hot (375°F, 190°C) cooking oil for about 2 minutes per batch until crisp and golden. Remove with slotted spoon to paper towels to drain. Makes 38 spring rolls.

1 spring roll: 52 Calories; 2.9 g Total Fat (1.6 g Mono, 0.9 g Poly, 0.2 g Sat); 3 mg Cholesterol; 5 g Carbohydrate; trace Fibre; 2 g Protein; 96 mg Sodium

Note: To cut chicken julienne, first place in the freezer for 30 minutes until the chicken is just beginning to freeze. Cut into 1/8 inch (3 mm) strips that resemble matchsticks.

Surprise Spread

First published in Appetizers, *this popular spread shows up at all the best parties! Serve with an assortment of tortilla chips or crackers.*

Block of cream cheese, softened	8 oz.	250 g
Sour cream	1/2 cup	125 mL
Salad dressing (or mayonnaise)	1/4 cup	60 mL
Bag of frozen cooked small shrimp (peeled and deveined), thawed	12 oz.	340 g
Seafood cocktail sauce	1 cup	250 mL
Grated mozzarella cheese	2 cups	500 mL
Diced green pepper	1 1/2 cups	375 mL
Green onions, sliced	3	3
Medium tomato, diced	1	1

Beat cream cheese, sour cream and salad dressing in small bowl until smooth. Spread evenly on extra-large serving platter or pizza pan, almost to edge.

Scatter shrimp over cream cheese mixture.

Layer remaining 5 ingredients, in order given, on top of shrimp. Cover. Chill until ready to serve. Serves 12.

1 serving: 228 Calories; 16.3 g Total Fat (5.3 g Mono, 1.5 g Poly, 8.5 g Sat); 100 mg Cholesterol; 8 g Carbohydrate; 1 g Fibre; 12 g Protein; 505 mg Sodium

Potluck Suggestion: Serves up to 16.

Cherry Surprise Muffins

Chocolate muffins with a cherry surprise in the centre, frosted with
scrumptious cherry-flavoured icing. Makes a great dessert.

All-purpose flour	1 3/4 cups	425 mL
Granulated sugar	1/2 cup	125 mL
Cocoa, sifted if lumpy	3 tbsp.	50 mL
Baking powder	1 tbsp.	15 mL
Salt	1/2 tsp.	2 mL
Large egg	1	1
Milk	3/4 cup	175 mL
Cooking oil	1/3 cup	75 mL
Vanilla	1 tsp.	5 mL
Block of cream cheese, softened	4 oz.	125 g
Granulated sugar	3 tbsp.	50 mL
Pitted Bing cherries, drained	12	12
CHERRY ICING		
Block of cream cheese, softened	4 oz.	125 g
Hard margarine (or butter), softened	1/4 cup	60 mL
Cherry brandy (or maraschino cherry syrup)	2 tsp.	10 mL
Icing (confectioner's) sugar	1 1/2 cups	375 mL
Chocolate curls (or grated chocolate)	1/4 cup	60 mL

Combine first 5 ingredients in large bowl. Make a well in centre.

Beat next 4 ingredients in small bowl. Add to well. Stir until just moistened.
Spoon 2 tbsp. (30 mL) batter into each of 12 greased muffin cups.

Beat cream cheese and second amount of sugar in same small bowl until
smooth. Spoon 2 tsp. (10 mL) cream cheese mixture on top of batter in
each muffin cup.

Place 1 cherry on top of cream cheese mixture in each. Spoon remaining
batter into muffin cups. Spread evenly to cover cream cheese mixture and
cherries. Bake in 400°F (205°C) oven for about 20 minutes until muffin
feels firm when pressed. Let stand in pan for 5 minutes before removing to
wire rack to cool completely.

(continued on next page)

Breads & Quick Breads

Cherry Icing: Beat cream cheese and margarine in small bowl until smooth. Add brandy. Beat well.

Add icing sugar 1/4 cup (60 mL) at a time, beating well after each addition until spreadable consistency. Makes about 1 1/4 cups (300 mL) icing. Spread 1 1/2 tbsp. (25 mL) icing on each muffin.

Sprinkle 1 tsp. (5 mL) chocolate curls on top of each muffin. Makes 12 muffins.

1 muffin: 378 Calories; 19.4 g Total Fat (9 g Mono, 2.7 g Poly, 6.6 g Sat); 42 mg Cholesterol; 47 g Carbohydrate; 1 g Fibre; 5 g Protein; 317 mg Sodium

Pictured on page 35.

Poppy Seed Loaf

Simple to make and full of flavour, this pretty loaf will be a welcome part of your next potluck. For more servings, cut each slice in half.

Large eggs	2	2
Granulated sugar	1 cup	250 mL
Milk	1 cup	250 mL
Cooking oil	1/2 cup	125 mL
Almond flavouring	1 tsp.	5 mL
Vanilla	1 tsp.	5 mL
All-purpose flour	2 cups	500 mL
Poppy seeds	2 tbsp.	30 mL
Baking powder	1 tsp.	5 mL
Salt	3/4 tsp.	4 mL

Beat eggs in large bowl until frothy. Add next 5 ingredients. Beat until smooth.

Combine remaining 4 ingredients in medium bowl. Add to egg mixture. Stir until just moistened. Spread evenly in greased 9 x 5 x 3 inch (22 x 12.5 x 7.5 cm) loaf pan. Bake in 350°F (175°C) oven for about 1 hour until wooden pick inserted in centre comes out clean. Let stand in pan for 10 minutes before removing to wire rack to cool. Cuts into 16 slices.

1 slice: 198 Calories; 8.7 g Total Fat (4.6 g Mono, 2.6 g Poly, 0.9 g Sat); 28 mg Cholesterol; 27 g Carbohydrate; 1 g Fibre; 3 g Protein; 151 mg Sodium

Pictured on page 35.

Sourdough Parmesan Bread

*Soft, fragrant sourdough bread studded with flecks of Parmesan cheese.
Make the starter two days before baking the loaves. Fine-textured loaves that
look good and taste great, especially served at a soup and salad potluck.*

Active dry yeast	1 tsp.	5 mL
Warm water	1 cup	250 mL
All-purpose flour	1 cup	250 mL
Warm water	3/4 cup	175 mL
Grated Parmesan cheese	1/3 cup	75 mL
Skim milk powder	2 tbsp.	30 mL
Hard margarine (or butter), melted	1 tbsp.	15 mL
Granulated sugar	1 tbsp.	15 mL
Salt	3/4 tsp.	4 mL
All-purpose flour	3 cups	750 mL
All-purpose flour, approximately	1/4 cup	60 mL
Yellow cornmeal	1 tsp.	5 mL
Water		

Sprinkle yeast over first amount of warm water in small bowl. Let stand for
10 minutes. Stir.

Measure first amount of flour into large bowl. Make a well in centre. Add
yeast mixture to well. Stir until smooth batter forms. Cover loosely with
plastic wrap. Let stand for 48 hours at warm room temperature (see Note),
stirring twice. Mixture will be bubbly and have a yeasty aroma.

Add next 6 ingredients. Stir.

Add second amount of flour. Mix until soft dough forms. Turn out onto
lightly floured surface. Knead for 5 to 10 minutes, adding third amount
of flour 1 tbsp. (15 mL) at a time if necessary to prevent sticking, until
smooth and elastic. Place in greased extra-large bowl, turning once to
grease top. Cover with greased waxed paper and tea towel. Let stand in
oven with light on and door closed for about 1 1/2 hours until doubled
in bulk. Punch dough down. Turn out onto lightly floured surface. Knead
for about 1 minute until smooth. Divide into 2 equal portions. Roll each
portion into ball.

(continued on next page)

Breads & Quick Breads

Sprinkle cornmeal on greased baking sheet. Arrange balls about 2 inches (5 cm) apart on top of cornmeal. Cover with greased waxed paper and tea towel. Let stand in oven with light on and door closed for about 45 minutes until doubled in size. Cut three 2 inch (5 cm) long slashes across top of each loaf.

Mist loaves with water. Bake in 350°F (175°C) oven for 35 to 40 minutes until golden brown and hollow sounding when tapped. Makes 2 loaves. Each loaf cuts into 12 slices, for a total of 24 slices.

1 slice: 101 Calories; 1.2 g Total Fat (0.5 g Mono, 0.2 g Poly, 0.4 g Sat); 1 mg Cholesterol; 19 g Carbohydrate; 1 g Fibre; 3 g Protein; 111 mg Sodium

Pictured on page 36.

Note: The top of your refrigerator or freezer is a good place to set the bowl for a consistent, warm temperature. Or, if your home is usually very warm, let it stand on the countertop.

Potluck Suggestion: For a large gathering, cut each slice in half.

SOURDOUGH PARMESAN BUNS: Divide entire amount of dough into 4 equal portions. Divide each portion into 6 equal pieces. Roll each piece into ball.

Sprinkle 2 greased baking sheets with cornmeal. Arrange 12 balls about 1 inch (2.5 cm) apart on top of cornmeal on each. Cover loosely with greased plastic wrap. Let stand in oven with light on and door closed for about 30 minutes until doubled in size.

Mist buns with water. Cut 2 inch (5 cm) long slash across top of each bun. Bake in 350°F (175°C) oven for about 30 minutes until golden brown and hollow sounding when tapped. Let stand on baking sheets for 5 minutes before removing to wire racks to cool. Makes 2 dozen (24) buns.

Paré Pointer
The best way to fire a math teacher is to tell him that he's history.

Lucky Day Rolls

These eye-catching, four-leaf clover rolls will be sure to please at any potluck.

All-purpose flour	2 cups	500 mL
Warm water	1/2 cup	125 mL
Granulated sugar	2 tbsp.	30 mL
Envelope of active dry yeast	1/4 oz.	8 g
(or 2 1/4 tsp., 11 mL)		
Large egg	1	1
Warm milk	3/4 cup	175 mL
Cooking oil	1/4 cup	60 mL
Salt	1 tsp.	5 mL
All-purpose flour	1 1/2 cups	375 mL
All-purpose flour, approximately	3 tbsp.	50 mL
Hard margarine (or butter), melted	1/4 cup	60 mL

Measure first amount of flour into large bowl. Make a well in centre.

Stir warm water and sugar in small bowl until sugar is dissolved. Sprinkle yeast over top. Let stand for 10 minutes. Stir until yeast is dissolved. Add to well.

Beat next 4 ingredients in same small bowl. Add to well. Stir until just moistened.

Add second amount of flour. Mix until soft dough forms. Turn out onto lightly floured surface. Knead for 5 to 10 minutes, adding third amount of flour 1 tbsp. (15 mL) at a time if necessary to prevent sticking, until smooth and elastic. Place in greased extra-large bowl, turning once to grease top. Cover with greased waxed paper and tea towel. Let stand in oven with light on and door closed for about 1 hour until doubled in bulk. Punch dough down. Turn out onto lightly floured surface. Knead for about 1 minute until smooth. Divide into 4 equal portions. Divide each portion into 6 equal pieces. Divide each piece into 4 equal portions. Roll each portion into ball. Arrange 4 balls, just touching, in each of 24 greased muffin cups. Cover with greased waxed paper and tea towel. Let stand in oven with light on and door closed until doubled in size. Bake in 400°F (205°C) oven for about 15 minutes until golden.

Brush tops of rolls with margarine. Let stand in pans for 5 minutes before removing to wire racks to cool. Makes 24 rolls.

1 roll: 125 Calories; 5 g Total Fat (2.9 g Mono, 1 g Poly, 0.7 g Sat); 9 mg Cholesterol; 17 g Carbohydrate; 1 g Fibre; 3 g Protein; 130 mg Sodium

Pictured on page 54.

Chocolate-Filled Rolls

Cinnamon buns with a chocolate twist. Make these when you're asked to bring a dessert to the potluck. Using frozen bread dough make these quick and easy to prepare.

Frozen white bread dough, covered and thawed in refrigerator overnight	1 lb.	454 g
Hard margarine (or butter), melted	1 1/2 tbsp.	25 mL
Brown sugar, packed	1/4 cup	60 mL
Cocoa, sifted if lumpy	1 tbsp.	15 mL
Ground cinnamon	1 tsp.	5 mL
Mini semi-sweet chocolate chips	3/4 cup	175 mL
Finely chopped pecans (or walnuts)	1/2 cup	125 mL
CHOCOLATE GLAZE		
Icing (confectioner's) sugar	2/3 cup	150 mL
Milk	4 tsp.	20 mL
Cocoa, sifted if lumpy	2 tsp.	10 mL
Vanilla	1/8 tsp.	0.5 mL

Roll out dough on lightly floured surface to 12 x 14 inch (30 x 35 cm) rectangle. Brush margarine evenly on dough.

Combine brown sugar, cocoa and cinnamon in small bowl. Sprinkle over margarine.

Sprinkle chocolate chips and pecans on top of brown sugar mixture. Press down lightly. Roll up from short side, jelly roll-style. Press seam against roll to seal. Cut into 1 inch (2.5 cm) slices. Arrange, cut-side up, about 1/2 inch (12 mm) apart in greased 9 x 13 inch (22 x 33 cm) pan. Cover with greased waxed paper and tea towel. Let stand in oven with light on and door closed for about 1 1/2 hours until doubled in size. Bake in 350°F (175°C) oven for about 25 minutes until golden. Let stand in pan on wire rack for about 10 minutes until slightly cooled.

Chocolate Glaze: Combine all 4 ingredients in small bowl, adding more milk or icing sugar if necessary until barely pourable consistency. Drizzle over each roll in pan. Makes 12 rolls.

1 roll: 250 Calories; 9.8 g Total Fat (4.9 g Mono, 1.4 g Poly, 2.9 g Sat); 0 mg Cholesterol; 39 g Carbohydrate; 2 g Fibre; 4 g Protein; 225 mg Sodium

Pictured on page 35.

Spice-Of-Life Muffins

*Sugar and spice and flavours that are nice—this muffin is packed
with good things! Take to a brunch or picnic potluck.*

Large eggs	2	2
Milk	1/2 cup	125 mL
Cooking oil	1/4 cup	60 mL
Fancy (mild) molasses	3 tbsp.	50 mL
All-bran cereal	1 cup	250 mL
Chopped pitted dates	1/2 cup	125 mL
All-purpose flour	1 cup	250 mL
Brown sugar, packed	3/4 cup	175 mL
Quick-cooking rolled oats (not instant)	1/2 cup	125 mL
Wheat germ	1 tbsp.	15 mL
Baking powder	2 1/2 tsp.	12 mL
Ground cinnamon	1/2 tsp.	2 mL
Ground ginger	1/2 tsp.	2 mL
Ground nutmeg	1/4 tsp.	1 mL
Salt	1/4 tsp.	1 mL

Beat eggs in medium bowl until frothy. Add milk, cooking oil and molasses.
Beat until smooth. Add cereal and dates. Stir well. Let stand for 10 minutes.

Combine remaining 9 ingredients in large bowl. Make a well in centre. Add
date mixture to well. Stir until just moistened. Fill 12 greased muffin cups
3/4 full. Bake in 400°F (205°C) oven for about 15 minutes until wooden pick
inserted in centre of muffin comes out clean. Let stand in pan for 5 minutes
before removing to wire rack to cool. Makes 12 muffins.

*1 muffin: 225 Calories; 6.4 g Total Fat (3.3 g Mono, 1.7 g Poly, 0.8 g Sat); 36 mg Cholesterol;
41 g Carbohydrate; 4 g Fibre; 4 g Protein; 204 mg Sodium*

Pictured on page 53.

Paré Pointer
The only fish that a bird will land on is perch.

Breads & Quick Breads

Coconut Cranberry Muffins

This muffin's sweet, crispy exterior invites you into a delicate,
cake-like interior studded with cranberries. Delicious!

All-purpose flour	2 cups	500 mL
Chopped pecans	1/3 cup	75 mL
Medium unsweetened coconut	1/4 cup	60 mL
Baking powder	1 tbsp.	15 mL
Ground cinnamon	1 tsp.	5 mL
Baking soda	1/2 tsp.	2 mL
Salt	1/2 tsp.	2 mL
Large eggs	2	2
Buttermilk (or reconstituted from powder)	1 cup	250 mL
Granulated sugar	2/3 cup	150 mL
Dried cranberries	1/2 cup	125 mL
Cooking oil	1/3 cup	75 mL

Combine first 7 ingredients in large bowl. Make a well in centre.

Beat eggs in medium bowl until frothy. Add remaining 4 ingredients.
Mix until smooth. Add to well. Stir until just moistened. Fill 12 greased
muffin cups 3/4 full. Bake in 400°F (205°C) oven for 15 to 18 minutes until
wooden pick inserted in centre of muffin comes out clean. Let stand in
pan for 5 minutes before removing to wire rack to cool. Makes 12 muffins.

1 muffin: 248 Calories; 11.3 g Total Fat (5.7 g Mono, 2.7 g Poly, 2.2 g Sat); 37 mg Cholesterol;
33 g Carbohydrate; 2 g Fibre; 5 g Protein; 280 mg Sodium

Pictured on page 53.

Chocolate Banana Bread

Nothing draws them in like chocolate, especially in a fabulous banana loaf! Sure to become a potluck favourite!

Hard margarine (or butter), softened	1/2 cup	125 mL
Granulated sugar	2/3 cup	150 mL
Large eggs	2	2
Mashed banana (about 3 medium)	1 cup	250 mL
Vanilla	1 tsp.	5 mL
All-purpose flour	2 cups	500 mL
Mini semi-sweet chocolate chips	1/2 cup	125 mL
Chopped walnuts (optional)	1/2 cup	125 mL
Cocoa, sifted if lumpy	2 tbsp.	30 mL
Baking powder	1 tsp.	5 mL
Baking soda	1 tsp.	5 mL
Salt	1/2 tsp.	2 mL

Cream margarine and sugar in large bowl. Add eggs 1 at a time, beating well after each addition. Add banana and vanilla. Beat well.

Combine remaining 7 ingredients in medium bowl. Add to banana mixture. Stir until just moistened. Spread evenly in greased 9 x 5 x 3 inch (22 x 12.5 x 7.5 cm) loaf pan. Bake in 350°F (175°C) oven for about 1 hour until wooden pick inserted in centre comes out clean. Let stand in pan for 10 minutes before removing to wire rack to cool. Cuts into 16 slices.

1 slice: 200 Calories; 8.6 g Total Fat (4.8 g Mono, 0.8 g Poly, 2.5 g Sat); 27 mg Cholesterol; 29 g Carbohydrate; 1 g Fibre; 3 g Protein; 257 mg Sodium

Pictured on page 35.

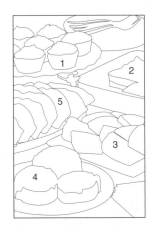

Coffee Potluck
1. Cherry Surprise Muffins, page 26
2. Bumbleberry Streusel Cake, page 136
3. Chocolate Banana Bread, above
4. Chocolate-Filled Rolls, page 31
5. Poppy Seed Loaf, page 27

Props courtesy of: Klass Works
                     Pfaltzgraff Canada

Pepper Cornbread Triangles

Moist and tender, with a peppery bite. Great with soups, stews or salads.

Yellow cornmeal	2 cups	500 mL
All-purpose flour	2 cups	500 mL
Granulated sugar	1/4 cup	60 mL
Baking powder	2 tbsp.	30 mL
Salt	1 1/2 tsp.	7 mL
Coarse ground pepper	2 tsp.	10 mL
Large eggs	3	3
Milk	2 cups	500 mL
Hard margarine (or butter), melted	1/4 cup	60 mL

Combine first 6 ingredients in large bowl. Make a well in centre.

Beat eggs, milk and margarine in small bowl until smooth. Add to well. Stir until just moistened. Spread evenly in greased 9 x 13 inch (22 x 33 cm) pan. Bake in 375°F (190°C) oven for about 25 minutes until edges are golden and wooden pick inserted in centre comes out clean. Cool. Make 2 lengthwise cuts about 3 inches (7.5 cm) apart. Make 3 crosswise cuts about 3 1/4 inches (8 cm) apart, for a total of 12 rectangles. Cut each rectangle in half diagonally. Makes 24 triangles.

1 triangle: 131 Calories; 3.2 g Total Fat (1.7 g Mono, 0.4 g Poly, 0.8 g Sat); 28 mg Cholesterol; 22 g Carbohydrate; 1 g Fibre; 4 g Protein; 284 mg Sodium

Pictured on page 107.

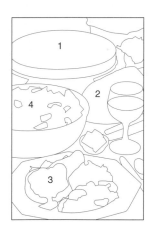

Potluck Dinner With Friends
1. Ginger Pear Cheesecake, page 138
2. Sourdough Parmesan Bread, page 28
3. Creamy Pork And Mushrooms, page 82
4. Orange Almond Salad, page 91

Props courtesy of: Casa Bugatti
Cherison Enterprises Inc.
Totally Bamboo

Flakes Of Oatmeal Bread

Deep golden bread sprinkled with flakes of oatmeal. Subtle molasses highlights the sweet, nutty flavour. A hearty bread to serve at any potluck.

Quick-cooking rolled oats (not instant)	1 1/2 cups	375 mL
Small can of evaporated milk	5 1/2 oz.	160 mL
Fancy (mild) molasses	1/3 cup	75 mL
Hard margarine (or butter)	2 tbsp.	30 mL
Salt	1 tsp.	5 mL
Hot water	2 cups	500 mL
Warm water	1/2 cup	125 mL
Granulated sugar	1 tsp.	5 mL
Envelope of active dry yeast	1/4 oz.	8 g
(or 2 1/4 tsp., 11 mL)		
All-purpose flour	5 1/2 cups	1.4 L
All-purpose flour, approximately	1/2 cup	125 mL
Large egg	1	1
Quick-cooking rolled oats (not instant)	1/3 cup	75 mL

Measure first 5 ingredients into extra-large bowl. Add hot water. Stir until margarine is melted. Cool to room temperature.

Stir warm water and sugar in small bowl until sugar is dissolved. Sprinkle yeast over top. Let stand for 10 minutes. Stir until yeast is dissolved. Add to rolled oats mixture. Stir.

Add first amount of flour. Mix until soft dough forms. Turn out onto lightly floured surface. Knead for 5 to 10 minutes, adding second amount of flour 1 tbsp. (15 mL) at a time if necessary to prevent sticking, until smooth and elastic. Place in greased extra-large bowl, turning once to grease top. Cover with greased waxed paper and tea towel. Let stand in oven with light on and door closed for about 1 1/2 hours until doubled in bulk. Punch dough down. Turn out onto lightly floured surface. Knead for about 1 minute until smooth. Divide into 2 equal portions. Roll each portion into ball.

(continued on next page)

Beat egg with fork in large shallow dish. Measure second amount of rolled oats into separate large shallow dish. Roll 1 ball in egg until coated. Press in rolled oats until coated. Place in greased 9 inch (22 cm) round pan. Repeat with second ball, placing in separate greased 9 inch (22 cm) round pan. Cover each pan with greased waxed paper and tea towel. Let stand in oven with light on and door closed for about 1 hour until doubled in size. Bake in 350°F (175°C) oven for 35 to 40 minutes until golden brown and hollow sounding when tapped. Let stand in pans for 5 minutes before removing to wire racks to cool. Makes 2 loaves. Each loaf cuts into 12 slices, for a total of 24 slices.

1 slice: 187 Calories; 2.6 g Total Fat (1.1 g Mono, 0.5 g Poly, 0.8 g Sat); 11 mg Cholesterol; 35 g Carbohydrate; 2 g Fibre; 5 g Protein; 123 mg Sodium

Potluck Suggestion: Use 1 loaf and freeze the other for your next potluck.

OATMEAL BUNS: Divide entire amount of dough into 4 equal portions. Divide each portion into 6 equal pieces. Roll each piece into ball.

Roll 1 ball in egg until coated. Press in rolled oats until coated. Repeat with remaining balls. Arrange 12 balls about 1 inch (2.5 cm) apart in greased 9 x 13 inch (22 x 33 cm) pan. Arrange remaining balls in separate greased 9 x 13 inch (22 x 33 cm) pan. Cover each pan with greased waxed paper and tea towel. Let stand in oven with light on and door closed for about 1 hour until doubled in size. Bake in 350°F (175°C) oven for about 20 minutes until golden brown and hollow sounding when tapped. Let stand in pans for 5 minutes before removing to wire racks to cool. Makes 2 dozen (24) buns.

Pictured on page 90.

Paré Pointer

If you had two banana peels, would you have a pair of slippers?

Pumpkin Pecan Loaf

A spicy loaf that might not make it to the potluck, it smells so good!
No problem—this recipe makes two loaves. Especially nice for a
Christmas or Thanksgiving gathering.

Large eggs	4	4
Granulated sugar	2 cups	500 mL
Can of pure pumpkin (no spices)	14 oz.	398 mL
Cooking oil	1 cup	250 mL
All-purpose flour	3 cups	750 mL
Chopped pecans	1 cup	250 mL
Baking powder	1 tsp.	5 mL
Baking soda	1 tsp.	5 mL
Ground cinnamon	1 tsp.	5 mL
Ground nutmeg	1 tsp.	5 mL
Salt	1 tsp.	5 mL
Ground cloves	1/2 tsp.	2 mL

Beat eggs in large bowl until frothy. Add sugar, pumpkin and cooking oil. Beat until smooth.

Combine remaining 8 ingredients in medium bowl. Add to pumpkin mixture. Stir until just moistened. Divide and spoon into 2 greased 9 x 5 x 3 inch (22 x 12.5 x 7.5 cm) loaf pans. Spread evenly. Bake in 350°F (175°C) oven for about 1 hour until wooden pick inserted in centre comes out clean. Let stand in pans for 10 minutes before removing to wire racks to cool. Makes 2 loaves. Each loaf cuts into 16 slices, for a total of 32 slices.

1 slice: 200 Calories; 10.6 g Total Fat (6.1 g Mono, 2.9 g Poly, 1 g Sat); 27 mg Cholesterol; 25 g Carbohydrate; 1 g Fibre; 3 g Protein; 135 mg Sodium

PUMPKIN PECAN MUFFINS: Fill 24 greased muffin cups 3/4 full. Bake in 375°F (190°C) oven for about 20 minutes until wooden pick inserted in centre of muffin comes out clean. Let stand in pans for 5 minutes before removing to wire racks to cool. Makes 2 dozen (24) muffins.

Pictured on page 71.

Zucchini Seed Bread

Great cinnamon flavour and just sweet enough to satisfy at the end of
a great potluck dinner. Batter bakes well in a loaf pan, if you prefer.
Just add 25 minutes to the baking time.

Large eggs	3	3
Granulated sugar	1 cup	250 mL
Hard margarine (or butter), melted	1/2 cup	125 mL
Vanilla	1 tsp.	5 mL
Grated zucchini (with peel)	1 1/2 cups	375 mL
Grated carrot	1/2 cup	125 mL
All-purpose flour	2 3/4 cups	675 mL
Shelled pumpkin seeds	1/4 cup	60 mL
Raw sunflower seeds	2 tbsp.	30 mL
Baking soda	1 tsp.	5 mL
Ground cinnamon	1 tsp.	5 mL
Baking powder	1/2 tsp.	2 mL
Salt	1/2 tsp.	2 mL

Beat eggs in large bowl until frothy. Add sugar, margarine and vanilla. Beat until smooth.

Add zucchini and carrot. Stir.

Combine remaining 7 ingredients in medium bowl. Add to zucchini mixture. Stir until just moistened. Spread evenly in greased 12 cup (3 L) bundt pan. Bake in 350°F (175°C) oven for about 50 minutes until wooden pick inserted in centre of bread comes out clean. Let stand in pan for 10 minutes before removing to wire rack to cool. Cuts into 16 slices.

1 slice: 225 Calories; 8.8 g Total Fat (4.8 g Mono, 1.7 g Poly, 1.8 g Sat); 40 mg Cholesterol; 32 g Carbohydrate; 2 g Fibre; 5 g Protein; 251 mg Sodium

Pictured on page 72.

Paré Pointer

The sea is full of seagulls, the bay is full of bagels.

Sesame Seafood Bows

A sweet vinaigrette finishes this Asian-inspired dish perfectly. Light, refreshing flavours make seafood a sensational addition to a brunch potluck.

Prepared chicken (or vegetable) broth	1/2 cup	125 mL
Dry white (or alcohol-free) wine	1/2 cup	125 mL
Bay leaf	1	1
Frozen uncooked large shrimp (peeled and deveined), thawed	1 lb.	454 g
Fresh (or frozen, thawed) large sea scallops, halved horizontally	7 oz.	200 g
Medium bow pasta (about 9 oz., 255 g)	3 cups	750 mL
Boiling water	9 cups	2.25 L
Salt	1 tsp.	5 mL
Sliced fresh white mushrooms	2 cups	500 mL
Snow peas, trimmed and cut diagonally into thin slices	2 cups	500 mL
Sliced red onion	1 1/2 cups	375 mL
Sliced red pepper	1 cup	250 mL
Can of sliced water chestnuts, drained	8 oz.	227 mL
SESAME VINAIGRETTE		
Rice (or white wine) vinegar	1/2 cup	125 mL
Sweet chili sauce	3 tbsp.	50 mL
Soy sauce	2 tbsp.	30 mL
Sesame oil, for flavour	2 tsp.	10 mL
Finely grated, peeled gingerroot (or 1/4 tsp., 1 mL, ground ginger)	1 tsp.	5 mL
Garlic clove, minced (or 1/4 tsp., 1 mL, powder)	1	1

Combine broth, wine and bay leaf in large pot or Dutch oven. Bring to a boil on medium. Add shrimp and scallops. Cover. Boil gently for about 3 minutes until shrimp turn pink and scallops are opaque. Discard bay leaf. Drain. Transfer to large bowl. Cool.

(continued on next page)

Cook pasta in boiling water and salt in same large uncovered pot or Dutch oven for 8 to 10 minutes, stirring occasionally, until tender but firm. Drain. Rinse with cold water until cool. Drain well. Add to seafood.

Add next 5 ingredients. Toss gently.

Sesame Vinaigrette: Combine all 6 ingredients in jar with tight-fitting lid. Shake well. Makes about 2/3 cup (150 mL) vinaigrette. Drizzle over pasta mixture. Toss gently. Serves 8.

1 serving: 277 Calories; 3 g Total Fat (0.7 g Mono, 1.2 g Poly, 0.5 g Sat); 73 mg Cholesterol; 40 g Carbohydrate; 3 g Fibre; 20 g Protein; 511 mg Sodium

Pictured on front cover.

Potluck Suggestion: Serves up to 16.

Paré Pointer
According to the height and weight chart, he should be nine feet tall.

Creamy Spinach Roulade

Creamy crab and herb filling spiralled into a soufflé-textured roll.
Delicious and impressive!

Hard margarine (or butter)	2 tbsp.	30 mL
Chopped onion	1 1/2 cups	375 mL
Boxes of frozen chopped spinach (10 oz., 300 g, each), thawed and squeezed dry	2	2
Large eggs, room temperature	4	4
All-purpose flour	1 cup	250 mL
Baking powder	2 tsp.	10 mL
Dill weed	1/2 tsp.	2 mL
Ground nutmeg	1/4 tsp.	1 mL
Salt	1/2 tsp.	2 mL
Pepper	1/8 tsp.	0.5 mL
Block of cream cheese, softened	8 oz.	250 g
Can of crabmeat, drained, cartilage removed (or imitation), flaked	6 oz.	170 g
Chopped fresh chives (or 3/4 tsp., 4 mL, dried)	1 tbsp.	15 mL
Chopped fresh parsley (or 3/4 tsp., 4 mL, flakes)	1 tbsp.	15 mL

Melt margarine in large frying pan on medium. Add onion. Cook for 5 to 10 minutes, stirring often, until softened.

Add spinach. Cook for 3 to 4 minutes, stirring occasionally, until liquid is evaporated. Cool.

Beat eggs in large bowl for about 5 minutes until frothy.

(continued on next page)

Brunches

Combine next 6 ingredients in small bowl. Fold into egg. Add spinach mixture. Fold in until just combined. Lightly grease bottom of 10 x 15 inch (25 x 38 cm) jelly roll pan. Line bottom with waxed paper. Spread egg mixture evenly in pan. Bake in 400°F (205°C) oven for about 12 minutes until wooden pick inserted in centre comes out clean. Run knife around inside edges of pan to loosen. Spread large tea towel on work surface. Cover towel with sheet of waxed paper. Invert roulade onto waxed paper. Discard top sheet of waxed paper. Roll up from short side, jelly roll-style, using bottom waxed paper and tea towel as guide. Cool.

Beat remaining 4 ingredients in same small bowl until well combined. Unroll roulade. Spread crab mixture evenly on top of roulade, almost to edges. Roll up from short side, jelly roll-style, to enclose filling, using waxed paper as guide. Wrap with same sheet of waxed paper and plastic wrap. Chill for about 2 hours until firm. Discard plastic wrap and waxed paper. Cut into 1/2 inch (12 mm) slices. Makes about 20 slices.

1 slice: 109 Calories; 6.8 g Total Fat (2.4 g Mono, 0.5 g Poly, 3.3 g Sat); 57 mg Cholesterol; 8 g Carbohydrate; 1 g Fibre; 5 g Protein; 224 mg Sodium

Pictured on page 53.

Paré Pointer
When bears lose their teeth, do they become gummy bears?

Chick And Leek Pie

A moist and tasty chicken pie that cuts into beautiful wedges. Treat your friends or family to this outstanding, savoury dish at your next brunch potluck.

Hard margarine (or butter)	2 tbsp.	30 mL
Medium leeks (white part only), thinly sliced	2	2
Brown sugar, packed	2 tsp.	10 mL
Finely chopped carrot	1 cup	250 mL
Finely chopped celery	1/2 cup	125 mL
Garlic cloves, minced (or 3/4 tsp., 4 mL, powder)	3	3
Salt	1/4 tsp.	1 mL
Pepper	1/8 tsp.	0.5 mL
All-purpose flour	2 tbsp.	30 mL
Prepared chicken broth	1 cup	250 mL
Dry white (or alcohol-free) wine	1/4 cup	60 mL
Chopped cooked chicken	3 cups	750 mL
Sour cream	1/4 cup	60 mL
Pastry for 2 crust 9 inch (22 cm) pie, your own or a mix		
Large egg, fork-beaten	1	1

Melt margarine in large frying pan on medium-low. Add leek. Cook for 15 to 20 minutes, stirring often, until caramelized.

Add brown sugar. Heat and stir for about 2 minutes until brown sugar is dissolved.

Add next 5 ingredients. Heat and stir for about 5 minutes until carrot and celery are softened. Increase heat to medium.

Add flour. Heat and stir for 1 minute. Slowly add broth and wine, stirring constantly. Heat and stir for 5 to 7 minutes until boiling and thickened.

Add chicken and sour cream. Stir well. Cool.

(continued on next page)

Divide pastry into 2 portions, 1 slightly larger than the other. Roll out larger portion on lightly floured surface to about 1/8 inch (3 mm) thickness. Line 9 inch (22 cm) pie plate. Spread chicken mixture evenly in pie shell. Roll out remaining pastry on lightly floured surface to about 1/8 inch (3 mm) thickness. Brush edge of pie shell with egg. Cover pie with remaining pastry. Trim and crimp decorative edge to seal. Brush top of pie with egg. Cut 2 or 3 small slits in top to allow steam to escape. Bake on bottom rack in 375°F (190°C) oven for about 50 minutes until pastry is golden. Let stand on wire rack for 10 minutes. Cuts into 6 wedges.

1 wedge: 488 Calories; 26 g Total Fat (12 g Mono, 3.7 g Poly, 8 g Sat); 107 mg Cholesterol; 34 g Carbohydrate; 2 g Fibre; 27 g Protein; 658 mg Sodium

Pictured on page 54.

Potluck Suggestion: Cut into 10 wedges.

 Provide enough plates, glasses, napkins and cutlery for your potluck. Have extra serving utensils available for those who don't bring them. The host usually provides any condiments as well.

Bean-Stuffed Peppers

Attractive red peppers stuffed with a black bean and rice filling.

Bacon slices, diced	4	4
Chopped onion	1/2 cup	125 mL
Chopped celery	1/2 cup	125 mL
Garlic clove, minced (or 1/4 tsp., 1 mL, powder)	1	1
Large egg	1	1
Sweet (or regular) chili sauce	2 tbsp.	30 mL
Can of black beans, rinsed and drained	19 oz.	540 mL
Cooked rice (about 1/3 cup, 75 mL, uncooked)	1 cup	250 mL
Medium tomato, diced	1	1
Salt, sprinkle		
Pepper, sprinkle		
Large red (or green) peppers, quartered lengthwise, seeds and ribs removed	3	3
Prepared chicken broth	1/3 cup	75 mL
Coarsely crushed tortilla chips	1 cup	250 mL
Grated sharp Cheddar cheese	1 cup	250 mL

Cook bacon in large frying pan until almost crisp. Discard drippings, reserving about 1 tbsp. (15 mL) in pan.

Add onion, celery and garlic. Cook on medium for 5 to 10 minutes, stirring often, until onion is softened and bacon is crisp.

Beat egg and chili sauce with fork in medium bowl.

Add bacon mixture and next 5 ingredients. Stir.

Spoon bean mixture into each red pepper piece. Arrange in single layer in ungreased 9 x 13 inch (22 x 33 cm) pan. Pour broth into pan around red pepper pieces. Cover with foil. Bake in 350°F (175°C) oven for 30 to 40 minutes until red pepper is tender-crisp. Remove from oven. Discard foil.

Combine tortilla chips and cheese in small bowl. Sprinkle over bean mixture in each red pepper piece. Bake, uncovered, for about 10 minutes until cheese is melted. Makes 12 stuffed peppers.

(continued on next page)

Brunches

Pictured on page 107.

Bacon Sour Cream Quiche

Everyone will love the familiar flavours of potato, bacon and sour cream in this brunch entrée. Quick and easy to prepare.

Hard margarine (or butter)	1/2 cup	125 mL
All-purpose flour	1 cup	250 mL
Frozen shredded hash brown potatoes	1/2 cup	125 mL
Grated medium Cheddar cheese	1/2 cup	125 mL
Worcestershire sauce	1/2 tsp.	2 mL
Salt	1/2 tsp.	2 mL
Onion powder	1/4 tsp.	1 mL
Bacon slices, diced	8	8
Grated Swiss cheese	1 cup	250 mL
Finely chopped green onion	1/3 cup	75 mL
Large eggs	3	3
Sour cream	1 1/2 cups	375 mL
All-purpose flour	1 tbsp.	15 mL
Salt	1/2 tsp.	2 mL
Pepper	1/8 tsp.	0.5 mL
Ground nutmeg	1/8 tsp.	0.5 mL

Melt margarine in large saucepan on medium. Remove from heat. Add next 6 ingredients. Stir well. Press firmly in bottom and up side of 9 inch (22 cm) pie plate. Set aside.

Cook bacon in medium frying pan until crisp. Transfer with slotted spoon to paper towels to drain. Scatter bacon over crust.

Sprinkle Swiss cheese over bacon. Sprinkle onion over top.

Beat remaining 6 ingredients in medium bowl until smooth. Pour over onion. Bake on bottom rack in 375°F (190°C) oven for about 40 minutes until knife inserted in centre comes out clean. Cuts into 6 wedges.

Potluck Suggestion: Cut into 10 wedges.

Pineapple Orange Crêpes

Delicate, orange-scented crêpes topped with a sweet, chunky sauce. Life is short—host a brunch potluck and invite your friends to eat dessert first!

ORANGE CRÊPES

All-purpose flour	1 cup	250 mL
Granulated sugar	1 tbsp.	15 mL
Salt	1/8 tsp.	0.5 mL
Large eggs	3	3
Milk	1 1/2 cups	375 mL
Hard margarine (or butter), melted	1/4 cup	60 mL
Grated orange peel	1/2 tsp.	2 mL
Hard margarine (or butter), approximately	2 tbsp.	30 mL

PINEAPPLE SAUCE

Reserved pineapple juice	1 cup	250 mL
Cornstarch	1 1/2 tbsp.	25 mL
Can of crushed pineapple, drained and juice reserved	19 oz.	540 mL
Orange juice	1/3 cup	75 mL
Liquid honey	1/3 cup	75 mL
Hard margarine (or butter)	2 tbsp.	30 mL
Ground cinnamon	1/4 tsp.	1 mL
Salt	1/8 tsp.	0.5 mL

Orange Crêpes: Combine flour, sugar and salt in large bowl. Make a well in centre.

Beat next 4 ingredients in small bowl until well combined. Add to well. Beat with whisk until smooth. Let stand for 1 hour. Stir. Makes about 2 3/4 cups (675 mL) batter.

Melt 1/4 tsp. (1 mL) of second amount of margarine in small (8 inch, 20 cm) non-stick frying pan on medium. Measure 2 1/2 tbsp. (37 mL) batter into 1/4 cup (60 mL) measure. Pour into pan. Immediately swirl batter to coat bottom, lifting and tilting pan to ensure entire bottom is covered. Cook for 1 to 1 1/2 minutes until top is set. Turn crêpe over. Cook for about 1 minute until brown spots appear on bottom. Remove to large plate. Cover to keep warm. Repeat with remaining batter, adding more margarine if necessary to prevent sticking. Makes about 16 crêpes.

(continued on next page)

Pineapple Sauce: Stir pineapple juice into cornstarch in medium saucepan until smooth.

Add remaining 6 ingredients. Stir. Cook on medium for 5 to 10 minutes, stirring occasionally, until boiling and thickened. Remove from heat. Makes about 2 2/3 cups (650 mL) sauce. Spread 1 cup (250 mL) sauce in ungreased 3 quart (3 L) shallow baking dish. Fold each crêpe in half, then in half again. Arrange, slightly overlapping, on top of sauce. Drizzle remaining sauce over crêpes. Serves 8.

1 serving: 327 Calories; 14.5 g Total Fat (8.6 g Mono, 1.5 g Poly, 3.4 g Sat); 83 mg Cholesterol; 45 g Carbohydrate; 1 g Fibre; 6 g Protein; 266 mg Sodium

Pictured on page 53.

Potluck Suggestion: Serves up to 16.

Paré Pointer

If only Noah had swatted the two mosquitoes.

Spinach Feta Pie

Who needs a crust? Spinach, mildly accented with flavourful feta cheese, forms the base of this delicious, golden-topped pie.

Box of frozen chopped spinach, thawed and squeezed dry	10 oz.	300 g
Crumbled feta cheese (about 2 1/2 oz., 70 g)	1/2 cup	125 mL
Block of light cream cheese, softened	8 oz.	250 g
Large eggs	6	6
Half-and-half cream (or homogenized milk)	1/2 cup	125 mL
Paprika	1/2 tsp.	2 mL
Pepper	1/2 tsp.	2 mL

Spread spinach evenly in greased 9 inch (22 cm) deep dish pie plate. Scatter feta cheese over top.

Beat cream cheese and 1 egg in medium bowl until smooth. Add remaining eggs 1 at a time, beating well after each addition.

Add cream, paprika and pepper. Stir well. Pour over feta cheese. Bake in 350°F (175°C) oven for about 45 minutes until knife inserted in centre comes out clean. Let stand for 10 minutes. Cuts into 8 wedges.

1 wedge: 180 Calories; 13.7 g Total Fat (4.2 g Mono, 0.9 g Poly, 7.2 g Sat); 195 mg Cholesterol; 4 g Carbohydrate; 1 g Fibre; 10 g Protein; 409 mg Sodium

Potluck Suggestion: Cut into 12 wedges.

Brunch Potluck
1. Coconut Cranberry Muffins, page 33
2. Pineapple Orange Crêpes, page 50
3. Spice-Of-Life Muffins, page 32
4. Creamy Spinach Roulade, page 44
5. Tomato Basil Pie, page 56

Props courtesy of: Canhome Global
Corelle®
Danesco Inc.
Pyrex® Originals

Hash Brown Skillet

Makes a hearty all-in-one brunch dish.

Cooking oil	1/2 tsp.	2 mL
Package of frozen sausage meat, thawed	13 oz.	375 g
Hard margarine (or butter)	2 tbsp.	30 mL
Frozen hash brown potatoes	4 cups	1 L
Grated carrot	1/2 cup	125 mL
Chopped onion	1/2 cup	125 mL
Diced green pepper	1/4 cup	60 mL
Finely diced pickled pepper rings	1 tbsp.	15 mL
Water	1 tbsp.	15 mL
Salt	3/4 tsp.	4 mL
Pepper	1/4 tsp.	1 mL
Large eggs	6	6
Grated medium Cheddar cheese	1 cup	250 mL

Heat cooking oil in large frying pan on medium. Add sausage. Scramble-fry for about 5 minutes until no longer pink. Transfer with slotted spoon to large bowl. Discard drippings.

Melt margarine in same large frying pan on medium-low. Add next 8 ingredients. Stir. Cover. Cook for 15 to 20 minutes, stirring often, until vegetables are tender and starting to brown. Spread evenly in pan.

Beat eggs in small bowl until frothy. Pour over potato mixture. Scatter sausage over egg. Sprinkle with cheese. Cover. Cook for about 5 minutes, without stirring, until egg is set. Remove to large serving plate. Cuts into 6 wedges.

1 wedge: 442 Calories; 27.5 g Total Fat (11.6 g Mono, 2.9 g Poly, 10.6 g Sat); 257 mg Cholesterol; 31 g Carbohydrate; 3 g Fibre; 19 g Protein; 818 mg Sodium

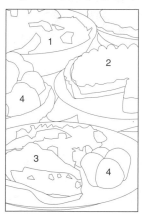

Summer Fun
1. Beef And Peanut Salad, page 96
2. Chocolate Raspberry Flan, page 134
3. Chick And Leek Pie, page 46
4. Lucky Day Rolls, page 30

Props courtesy of: Canhome Global
Danesco Inc.

Tomato Basil Pie

Firm-textured quiche accented with nutty Swiss cheese,
fresh tomato and basil. A delicious brunch potluck pie.

Hard margarine (or butter)	1 tbsp.	15 mL
Chopped green pepper	1 cup	250 mL
Chopped onion	1 cup	250 mL
Unbaked 9 inch (22 cm) pie shell	1	1
Large eggs	3	3
Mayonnaise (not salad dressing)	1/2 cup	125 mL
All-purpose flour	1 tbsp.	15 mL
Salt	1/2 tsp.	2 mL
Pepper	1/2 tsp.	2 mL
Fine dry bread crumbs	1/2 cup	125 mL
Finely shredded basil	3 tbsp.	50 mL
Medium tomatoes, cut into 1/4 inch (6 mm) slices	2	2
Swiss (or Monterey Jack) cheese, sliced and cut into wide strips	4 oz.	113 g

Melt margarine in medium frying pan on medium-high. Add green pepper and onion. Cook for 5 to 10 minutes, stirring often, until onion is softened. Cool slightly. Spread evenly in pie shell.

Beat next 5 ingredients in medium bowl until smooth. Pour over onion mixture. Spread evenly.

Sprinkle with bread crumbs and basil. Bake on bottom rack in 350°F (175°C) oven for about 30 minutes until starting to set. Remove from oven.

Layer tomato slices alternately with cheese strips, slightly overlapping, on top of pie. Bake for another 25 minutes until pastry is golden and cheese is melted. Let stand on wire rack for 10 minutes. Cuts into 8 wedges.

1 wedge: 334 Calories; 24.7 g Total Fat (11.8 g Mono, 5.3 g Poly, 6.3 g Sat); 102 mg Cholesterol; 19 g Carbohydrate; 1 g Fibre; 9 g Protein; 469 mg Sodium

Pictured on page 53.

Potluck Suggestion: Cut into 12 wedges.

Meatball Bake

Creamy rice topped with tender meatballs will chase away the cold.

Lean ground pork	1 lb.	454 g
Frozen pork sausage meat, thawed	6 oz.	170 g
Fine dry bread crumbs	1/2 cup	125 mL
Cooking oil	2 tsp.	10 mL
Chopped fresh white mushrooms	2 cups	500 mL
Diced onion	1 cup	250 mL
Diced green or red pepper	1/2 cup	125 mL
Water	2 cups	500 mL
Can of condensed cream of mushroom soup	10 oz.	284 mL
Milk	1/2 cup	125 mL
Instant rice	2 cups	500 mL
Grated medium Cheddar cheese	1/2 cup	125 mL
Salt	1/2 tsp.	2 mL
Pepper	1/8 tsp.	0.5 mL
Grated medium Cheddar cheese	1/2 cup	125 mL

Combine ground pork, sausage and bread crumbs in large bowl. Roll into 1 inch (2.5 cm) balls. Arrange in single layer in greased baking sheet with sides. Bake in 400°F (205°C) oven for 10 minutes. Transfer to paper towels to drain. Makes about 4 1/2 dozen (54) meatballs.

Heat cooking oil in large frying pan on medium. Add mushrooms, onion and green pepper. Cook for 5 to 10 minutes, stirring often, until onion is softened.

Combine water, soup and milk in separate large bowl.

Add onion mixture and next 4 ingredients. Stir well. Spread evenly in greased 2 1/2 quart (2.5 L) casserole. Arrange meatballs in single layer on top of rice mixture.

Sprinkle with second amount of cheese. Cover. Bake in 350°F (175°C) oven for 45 minutes. Remove cover. Bake for another 10 to 15 minutes until cheese is golden. Serves 6.

1 serving: 573 Calories; 31.7 g Total Fat (12.2 g Mono, 4.5 g Poly, 12.6 g Sat); 88 mg Cholesterol; 45 g Carbohydrate; 2 g Fibre; 26 g Protein; 972 mg Sodium

Potluck Suggestion: Serves up to 12.

Pastitsio

When it's all Greek to you, and everyone else too, this will fit in perfectly!
No need to wait for a theme potluck—Pah-STEET-see-oh is
a uniquely flavoured casserole that's great any time.

Olive (or cooking) oil	1 tbsp.	15 mL
Finely chopped onion	1 1/2 cups	375 mL
Ground cumin	1 tsp.	5 mL
Ground cinnamon	1 tsp.	5 mL
Lean ground beef	1 lb.	454 g
Prepared beef broth	1 cup	250 mL
Tomato paste (see Tip, page 59)	2 tbsp.	30 mL
Salt	1/4 tsp.	1 mL
Chopped fresh mint leaves (or 2 1/4 tsp., 11 mL, dried)	3 tbsp.	50 mL
Elbow macaroni	2 cups	500 mL
Boiling water	8 cups	2 L
Salt	1 tsp.	5 mL
Hard margarine (or butter)	1/4 cup	60 mL
All-purpose flour	1/4 cup	60 mL
Milk	1 1/2 cups	375 mL
Sour cream	1/3 cup	75 mL
Grated Parmesan cheese	1 cup	250 mL

Heat olive oil in large frying pan on medium. Add onion. Cook for 5 to 10 minutes, stirring often, until softened.

Add cumin and cinnamon. Heat and stir for about 1 minute until fragrant.

Add ground beef. Scramble-fry for 5 to 10 minutes until beef is no longer pink. Drain.

Add broth, tomato paste and first amount of salt. Stir. Bring to a boil. Reduce heat to medium-low. Simmer, uncovered, for about 10 minutes, stirring occasionally, until thickened.

(continued on next page)

Add mint. Stir. Remove from heat. Cover to keep warm.

Cook macaroni in boiling water and second amount of salt in large uncovered saucepan for 10 to 12 minutes until tender but firm. Drain. Transfer to large bowl. Set aside.

Melt margarine in same large saucepan on medium. Add flour. Heat and stir for 1 minute.

Slowly add milk, stirring constantly. Add sour cream. Heat and stir for about 2 minutes until boiling and thickened.

Add 1/2 cup (125 mL) Parmesan cheese. Stir. Remove from heat. Add macaroni. Stir until coated. Spread 1/2 of macaroni mixture evenly in greased 2 quart (2 L) casserole. Spread beef mixture on top. Spread remaining macaroni mixture on top of beef mixture. Sprinkle with remaining Parmesan cheese. Bake, uncovered, in 325°F (160°C) oven for about 55 minutes until heated through and Parmesan cheese is golden. Serves 6.

1 serving: 519 Calories; 25.5 g Total Fat (12.1 g Mono, 1.8 g Poly, 9.6 g Sat); 61 mg Cholesterol; 41 g Carbohydrate; 2 g Fibre; 30 g Protein; 734 mg Sodium

Potluck Suggestion: Serves up to 12.

 If a recipe calls for less than an entire can of tomato paste, freeze the unopened can for 30 minutes. Open both ends and push the contents through one end. Slice off only what you need. Freeze the remaining paste in a resealable freezer bag or plastic wrap for future use.

Layered Veggies And Rice

A delicious meatless dish. It tastes like lasagne, but it's made with rice instead of noodles and has a gooey cheese topping.

TOMATO SAUCE

Cooking oil	2 tbsp.	30 mL
Chopped onion	1/2 cup	125 mL
Chopped green pepper	1/2 cup	125 mL
Garlic clove, minced (or 1/4 tsp., 1 mL, powder)	1	1
Sliced fresh white mushrooms	2 cups	500 mL
Can of diced tomatoes (with juice)	14 oz.	398 mL
Can of tomato sauce	7 1/2 oz.	213 mL
Granulated sugar	1/2 tsp.	2 mL
Dried basil	1/2 tsp.	2 mL
Dried whole oregano	1/2 tsp.	2 mL
Pepper	1/4 tsp.	1 mL
Cooking oil	2 tsp.	10 mL
Grated carrot	1 1/4 cups	300 mL
Chopped onion	1/2 cup	125 mL
Chopped celery	1/4 cup	60 mL
Cold cooked long grain white rice (about 1 2/3 cups, 400 mL, uncooked)	5 cups	1.25 L
Package of ricotta cheese	16 oz.	500 g
Grated part-skim mozzarella cheese	1 cup	250 mL
Salt	1/4 tsp.	1 mL
Pepper	1/8 tsp.	0.5 mL
Grated part-skim mozzarella cheese	2 cups	500 mL

Tomato Sauce: Heat first amount of cooking oil in large saucepan on medium. Add first amount of onion, green pepper and garlic. Cook for about 5 minutes, stirring often, until onion starts to soften.

Add mushrooms. Cook for about 5 minutes, stirring often, until onion and mushrooms are softened.

(continued on next page)

Add next 6 ingredients. Stir. Bring to a boil. Reduce heat to medium-low. Simmer, uncovered, for about 15 minutes, stirring occasionally, until slightly thickened. Remove from heat. Cover to keep warm. Makes about 3 1/3 cups (825 mL) sauce.

Heat second amount of cooking oil in large frying pan on medium. Add carrot, second amount of onion and celery. Cook for 5 to 10 minutes, stirring often, until onion is softened. Remove from heat. Let stand for 10 minutes.

Combine next 5 ingredients in large bowl. Add carrot mixture. Stir well. Spread 1/2 of rice mixture evenly in greased 3 quart (3 L) shallow baking dish. Spread 1/2 of sauce on top of rice mixture. Repeat with remaining rice mixture and sauce.

Sprinkle with second amount of mozzarella cheese. Bake, uncovered, in 350°F (175°C) oven for 45 to 50 minutes until heated through and cheese is golden. Let stand for 10 minutes before cutting. Cuts into 8 pieces.

1 piece: 488 Calories; 20.8 g Total Fat (7.2 g Mono, 2.1 g Poly, 10.4 g Sat); 58 mg Cholesterol; 51 g Carbohydrate; 3 g Fibre; 24 g Protein; 604 mg Sodium

Pictured on page 108.

Potluck Suggestion: Cut into 16 pieces.

 When seating will be limited at your potluck, ask guests to bring a dish that requires only the use of a fork.

Rosemary Turkey Bake

A great dish to serve leftover turkey at a Boxing Day potluck.

Whole wheat spaghetti, broken up	8 oz.	225 g
Boiling water	8 cups	2 L
Salt	1 tsp.	5 mL
Cooking oil	2 tsp.	10 mL
Sliced fresh white mushrooms	3 cups	750 mL
Finely chopped onion	1/4 cup	60 mL
Prepared chicken broth	2 cups	500 mL
Can of skim evaporated milk	13 1/2 oz.	385 mL
All-purpose flour	3 tbsp.	50 mL
Diced cooked turkey	2 1/2 cups	625 mL
Medium sherry	3 tbsp.	50 mL
Finely chopped fresh rosemary leaves (or 1/4 tsp., 1 mL, dried, crushed)	1 tsp.	5 mL
Lemon pepper	1 tsp.	5 mL
Pepper	1/2 tsp.	2 mL
Grated Parmesan cheese	1/2 cup	125 mL
Paprika	1/2 tsp.	2 mL

Cook spaghetti in boiling water and salt in large uncovered pot or Dutch oven for 8 to 10 minutes, stirring occasionally, until tender but firm. Drain. Rinse with warm water. Drain well. Transfer to large bowl. Set aside.

Heat cooking oil in large frying pan on medium. Add mushrooms and onion. Cook for 5 to 10 minutes, stirring often, until onion is softened. Add broth. Stir. Bring to a boil. Boil gently, uncovered, for about 15 minutes until liquid is reduced by about half.

Stir evaporated milk into flour in small bowl until smooth. Slowly add to mushroom mixture, stirring constantly. Heat and stir for about 5 minutes until boiling and thickened.

Add next 5 ingredients. Stir well. Add to spaghetti. Toss until coated. Spread evenly in greased 2 1/2 quart (2.5 L) casserole. Cover. Bake in 350°F (175°C) oven for about 20 minutes until heated through. Remove from oven.

Sprinkle with Parmesan cheese and paprika. Bake, uncovered, for another 10 to 15 minutes until Parmesan cheese is golden. Serves 4.

(continued on next page)

Casseroles

1 serving: 569 Calories; 10.8 g Total Fat (3.5 g Mono, 2.1 g Poly, 4 g Sat); 106 mg Cholesterol; 64 g Carbohydrate; 6 g Fibre; 54 g Protein; 995 mg Sodium

Pictured on page 71.

Potluck Suggestion: Serves up to 8.

Oriental Rice Casserole

Crunchy noodles top this flavourful casserole. Take noodles separately to sprinkle over top just before dinner is served.

Cooking oil	2 tsp.	10 mL
Lean ground chicken (or turkey)	1 lb.	454 g
Chopped onion	1 cup	250 mL
Thinly sliced celery	1 cup	250 mL
Diced red pepper	1 cup	250 mL
Frozen peas, thawed	2 cups	500 mL
Fresh bean sprouts	1 1/2 cups	375 mL
Long grain white rice	1 1/2 cups	375 mL
Can of sliced mushrooms (with liquid)	10 oz.	284 mL
Soy sauce	3 tbsp.	50 mL
Can of condensed cream of mushroom soup	10 oz.	284 mL
Hot water	1 cup	250 mL
Oyster sauce	1 tbsp.	15 mL
Chinese five-spice powder	1/2 tsp.	2 mL
Pepper	1/2 tsp.	2 mL
Dry chow mein noodles	1 cup	250 mL

Heat cooking oil in large frying pan on medium-high. Add next 4 ingredients. Scramble-fry for 5 to 10 minutes until chicken is no longer pink. Drain.

Add next 5 ingredients. Stir. Remove from heat.

Combine next 5 ingredients in large bowl. Add chicken mixture. Stir well. Spread evenly in ungreased 4 quart (4 L) casserole. Cover. Bake in 350°F (175°C) oven for about 45 minutes, stirring once at halftime, until liquid is absorbed and rice is tender.

Just before serving, sprinkle with noodles. Serves 6.

1 serving: 520 Calories; 18.8 g Total Fat (2.4 g Mono, 3.9 g Poly, 1.7 g Sat); 1 mg Cholesterol; 64 g Carbohydrate; 6 g Fibre; 24 g Protein; 1387 mg Sodium

Potluck Suggestion: Serves up to 12.

Cheese And Pasta In A Pot

First published in Casseroles, *this dish is one of our favourite potluck pleasers. It can be prepared in the morning and chilled. Then, bake just before it's time to go or just before guests are scheduled to arrive.*

Large shell pasta	8 oz.	225 g
Boiling water	10 cups	2.5 L
Cooking oil	2 tsp.	10 mL
Lean ground beef	2 lbs.	900 g
Chopped onion	1 1/2 cups	375 mL
Tomato pasta sauce	1 2/3 cups	400 mL
Can of stewed tomatoes (with juice)	14 oz.	398 mL
Can of mushroom stems and pieces (with liquid)	10 oz.	284 mL
Garlic powder	1/4 tsp.	1 mL
Sour cream	2 cups	500 mL
Medium Cheddar cheese, cut into thin slices	1/2 lb.	225 g
Mozzarella cheese, cut into thin slices	1/2 lb.	225 g

Cook pasta in boiling water in large uncovered pot or Dutch oven for 10 to 12 minutes, stirring occasionally, until tender but firm. Drain. Rinse with cold water. Drain well. Transfer to large bowl. Set aside.

Heat cooking oil in same large pot on medium. Add ground beef and onion. Scramble-fry for 5 to 10 minutes until beef is no longer pink. Drain.

Add next 4 ingredients. Stir. Bring to a boil. Reduce heat to medium-low. Simmer, uncovered, for about 20 minutes, stirring occasionally, until slightly thickened. Remove from heat.

(continued on next page)

Layer ingredients in greased 4 quart (4 L) casserole or medium roasting pan as follows:

1. 1/2 of pasta, spread evenly

2. 1/2 of meat sauce

3. 1/2 of sour cream

4. 1/2 of Cheddar cheese slices

5. Remaining pasta

6. Remaining meat sauce

7. Remaining sour cream

8. Remaining Cheddar cheese slices

9. Mozzarella cheese slices

Cover. Bake in 350°F (175°C) oven for 45 minutes. Remove cover. Bake for another 5 to 10 minutes until cheese is melted and golden. Serves 12.

1 serving: 443 Calories; 25.2 g Total Fat (8.8 g Mono, 1.6 g Poly, 12.9 g Sat); 90 mg Cholesterol; 27 g Carbohydrate; 2 g Fibre; 27 g Protein; 574 mg Sodium

Potluck Suggestion: Serves up to 24.

Paré Pointer

The turkey couldn't eat any more. He was stuffed.

Oven-Braised Steak Rolls

A little bit of horseradish makes these rouladen-style rolls
extra zesty. Everyone's sure to love them!

Dijon mustard	3 tbsp.	50 mL
Creamed horseradish	1 tbsp.	15 mL
Pepper	1/4 tsp.	1 mL
Rouladen steaks, about 1/4 inch (6 mm) thick (about 2 lbs., 900 g)	8	8
Chopped onion	1 cup	250 mL
Bacon slices, halved	4	4
Dill pickles (4 inches, 10 cm, each), quartered lengthwise	2	2
Can of condensed beef (or vegetable) broth	10 oz.	284 mL
Water	1/2 cup	125 mL
Dried thyme	1/2 tsp.	2 mL
Bay leaf	1	1
Hard margarine (or butter)	2 tbsp.	30 mL
All-purpose flour	3 tbsp.	50 mL

Combine mustard, horseradish and pepper in small bowl. Spread on 1 side of each steak.

Sprinkle about 2 tbsp. (30 mL) onion over mustard mixture on each.

Place 1 bacon slice half across centre of each steak.

Place 1 pickle slice across bottom of each steak, about 1/2 inch (12 mm) from edge. Roll up tightly from bottom to enclose filling. Secure with wooden picks. Arrange rolls, seam-side down, in greased 2 quart (2 L) casserole.

Combine broth, water and thyme in 2 cup (500 mL) liquid measure. Pour over rolls. Add bay leaf. Cover. Bake in 350°F (175°C) oven for 1 1/2 to 2 hours until steak is tender. Discard bay leaf. Transfer rolls with slotted spoon to large plate. Transfer broth mixture from casserole to separate 2 cup (500 mL) liquid measure. Discard wooden picks from rolls. Return rolls to casserole, seam-side down. Cover to keep warm. Skim fat from broth mixture.

(continued on next page)

Casseroles

Melt margarine in medium saucepan on medium. Add flour. Heat and stir for 3 to 4 minutes until golden. Slowly add broth mixture, stirring constantly until boiling. Reduce heat to medium-low. Simmer for about 5 minutes, stirring often, until thickened. Pour over rolls. Serves 8.

1 serving: 175 Calories; 10.1 g Total Fat (4.8 g Mono, 1 g Poly, 3.4 g Sat); 27 mg Cholesterol; 5 g Carbohydrate; 1 g Fibre; 15 g Protein; 643 mg Sodium

Potluck Suggestion: Cut cooked rolls in half to serve up to 16.

Chicken And Corn Bake

This tasty dish will quickly become a potluck favourite.

Cans of cream-style corn (14 oz., 398 mL, each)	2	2
Frozen kernel corn	1 cup	250 mL
Milk	1 cup	250 mL
Chopped green onion	1/3 cup	75 mL
All-purpose flour	1/4 cup	60 mL
Large eggs	2	2
Chicken drumsticks (4 – 6 oz., 113 – 170 g, each), skin removed	12	12
Salt	1/2 tsp.	2 mL
Pepper	1/4 tsp.	1 mL
Hard margarine (or butter)	2 tbsp.	30 mL
Soda cracker crumbs	1/2 cup	125 mL
Paprika	1/4 tsp.	1 mL

Combine first 6 ingredients in large bowl. Spread evenly in ungreased 3 quart (3 L) casserole.

Arrange drumsticks in single layer on top of corn mixture. Sprinkle with salt and pepper.

Melt margarine in small saucepan. Add cracker crumbs and paprika. Mix well. Sprinkle over drumsticks. Cover. Bake in 350°F (175°C) oven for 30 minutes. Remove cover. Bake for another 1 to 1 1/2 hours until chicken is tender. Serves 6.

1 serving: 421 Calories; 14.3 g Total Fat (6 g Mono, 2.8 g Poly, 3.6 g Sat); 167 mg Cholesterol; 45 g Carbohydrate; 2 g Fibre; 32 g Protein; 789 mg Sodium

Potluck Suggestion: One drumstick per person, serves 12.

Ginger Cabbage Rolls

Tangy, sweet and sour flavours are a nice surprise in these tasty bundles.
Ready to go, right in the slow cooker.

Large head of green cabbage (about 4 1/2 lbs., 2 kg)	1	1
Boiling water		
Large egg	1	1
Lean ground beef	1 lb.	454 g
Cooked long grain white rice (about 1/3 cup, 75 mL, uncooked)	1 cup	250 mL
Lean ground pork	1/2 lb.	225 g
Salt	3/4 tsp.	4 mL
Pepper	1/2 tsp.	2 mL
Ground nutmeg	1/4 tsp.	1 mL
Can of tomato sauce	14 oz.	398 mL
Chopped onion	1 cup	250 mL
White vinegar	3 tbsp.	50 mL
Brown sugar, packed	2 tbsp.	30 mL
Ground ginger	1/2 tsp.	2 mL
Salt	1/4 tsp.	1 mL
Pepper	1/4 tsp.	1 mL
Gingersnaps, crushed, for garnish	3	3

Put cabbage into deep extra-large bowl or large pot. Pour boiling water over top until covered. Cover bowl with foil. Let stand for 5 minutes. Drain. Let stand until cool enough to handle. Carefully remove 8 large outer leaves from cabbage head (see Note). Cut 'V' shape with knife along tough rib of each cabbage leaf to remove. Discard ribs.

Combine next 7 ingredients in large bowl. Spoon onto centre of each cabbage leaf. Fold sides over filling. Roll up tightly from bottom to enclose.

Combine next 7 ingredients in 3 1/2 to 4 quart (3.5 to 4 L) slow cooker. Arrange cabbage rolls in 2 layers, seam-side down, on top of sauce. Cover. Cook on Low for 8 to 9 hours or on High for 4 to 4 1/2 hours.

Just before serving, garnish with crushed gingersnaps. Serves 8.

(continued on next page)

Main Dishes

1 serving: *329 Calories; 15.9 g Total Fat (6.7 g Mono, 1.3 g Poly, 6 g Sat); 79 mg Cholesterol; 28 g Carbohydrate; 5 g Fibre; 21 g Protein; 708 mg Sodium*

Pictured on page 90.

Note: Discard any outer leaves that are partially steamed. Chill the remaining head of cabbage and use it to make your favourite coleslaw.

Potluck Suggestion: Cut cooked rolls in half and arrange in a serving dish. Spoon sauce from the slow cooker over top to serve up to 16.

Paré Pointer
Old history teachers never marry—they just get dated.

Swiss Stew

This recipe made its debut in Casseroles.
*It's good any time, but makes an especially
warming dish for a winter potluck.*

Cooking oil	2 tbsp.	30 mL
Inside round steak, cut into 8 equal pieces	2 lbs.	900 g
Garlic powder, sprinkle		
Salt, sprinkle		
Pepper, sprinkle		
Can of stewed tomatoes (with juice)	14 oz.	398 mL
Can of mushroom stems and pieces (with liquid)	10 oz.	284 mL
Coarsely chopped onion	3/4 cup	175 mL
Can of tomato paste	5 1/2 oz.	156 mL
Celery ribs, cut into 2 inch (5 cm) pieces	4 – 6	4 – 6

Heat 1 tbsp. (15 mL) cooking oil in large frying pan on medium. Add
1/2 of steak pieces. Sprinkle with garlic powder, salt and pepper. Cook for
3 to 4 minutes per side until browned. Transfer to ungreased 3 quart (3 L)
casserole or small roasting pan. Repeat with remaining cooking oil, steak
and seasonings.

Combine remaining 5 ingredients in large bowl. Pour over steak. Cover.
Bake in 350°F (175°C) oven for 2 to 2 1/2 hours until steak is tender.
Serves 8.

*1 serving: 228 Calories; 8.6 g Total Fat (4.1 g Mono, 1.4 g Poly, 2.2 g Sat); 50 mg Cholesterol;
11 g Carbohydrate; 3 g Fibre; 27 g Protein; 328 mg Sodium*

Potluck Suggestion: Cut steak into 12 equal pieces to serve 12.

Holiday Potluck
1. Peach And Fennel Salad, page 101
2. Pumpkin Pecan Muffins, page 40
3. Pear Flower Gingerbread, page 133
4. Rosemary Turkey Bake, page 62

Props courtesy of: Corningware®
                  Danesco Inc.
                  Strahl

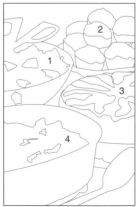

Cranberry Meatballs

First published in Millennium Edition, *these tasty meatballs have proven to be an excellent potluck choice any time of year. Easy to double for larger crowds.*

Large eggs, fork-beaten	2	2
Cornflake crumbs	1 cup	250 mL
Finely chopped onion	1/2 cup	125 mL
Soy sauce	2 tbsp.	30 mL
Parsley flakes	1 tbsp.	15 mL
Salt	2 tsp.	10 mL
Pepper	1/2 tsp.	2 mL
Garlic powder	1/2 tsp.	2 mL
Lean ground beef	2 lbs.	900 g
Can of cranberry sauce	14 oz.	398 mL
Chili sauce	1/2 cup	125 mL
Ketchup	1/2 cup	125 mL
Brown sugar, packed	2 tbsp.	30 mL
White vinegar	1 tbsp.	15 mL

Combine first 8 ingredients in large bowl. Add ground beef. Mix well. Roll into 1 inch (2.5 cm) balls. Place in ungreased 3 quart (3 L) casserole.

Combine remaining 5 ingredients in small bowl. Pour over meatballs. Bake, uncovered, in 350°F (175°C) oven for about 1 1/2 hours until meatballs are no longer pink inside. Serves 8.

1 serving: 454 Calories; 18.5 g Total Fat (7.9 g Mono, 0.9 g Poly, 7.2 g Sat); 117 mg Cholesterol; 47 g Carbohydrate; 2 g Fibre; 25 g Protein; 1515 mg Sodium

Potluck Suggestion: Serves up to 20.

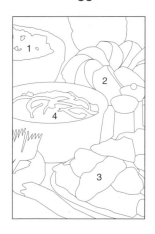

Picnic Potluck
1. Dilled Potato Salad, page 92
2. Zucchini Seed Bread, page 41
3. Easy Crispy Chicken, page 77
4. Marinated Cucumbers, page 105

Props courtesy of: Corningware®

Main Dishes

Chili Beef Stew

This colourful stew is great potluck fare for a casual crowd.

All-purpose flour	2 tbsp.	30 mL
Pepper	1/2 tsp.	2 mL
Beef stew meat, cut into small cubes	1 lb.	454 g
Cooking oil	1 tbsp.	15 mL
Cooking oil	1 tbsp.	15 mL
Sliced fresh white mushrooms	1 1/2 cups	375 mL
Chopped onion	1 cup	250 mL
Diced peeled potato	1 cup	250 mL
Chili powder	2 tsp.	10 mL
Ground cumin	2 tsp.	10 mL
Garlic clove, minced (or 1/4 tsp., 1 mL, powder)	1	1
Prepared beef broth	2 cups	500 mL
Can of diced tomatoes (with juice)	14 oz.	398 mL
Chopped green pepper	1 cup	250 mL
Can of diced green chilies	4 oz.	113 g
Can of white kidney beans, rinsed and drained	19 oz.	540 mL
Can of kernel corn, drained	12 oz.	341 mL

Combine flour and pepper in large resealable freezer bag. Add beef. Seal bag. Toss until coated. Heat first amount of cooking oil in large pot or Dutch oven on medium-high. Add beef. Cook for 5 to 10 minutes, stirring occasionally, until browned. Transfer to medium bowl.

Heat second amount of cooking oil in same large pot. Add next 6 ingredients. Stir. Cook for about 5 minutes, stirring occasionally and scraping any brown bits from bottom of pan, until onion starts to soften.

Slowly add broth, stirring constantly. Bring to a boil. Add beef and next 3 ingredients. Stir. Reduce heat to medium-low. Cover. Simmer for about 1 1/2 hours until beef is tender.

Add beans and corn. Stir. Simmer, uncovered, for about 5 minutes until heated through. Serves 6.

1 serving: 339 Calories; 12.5 g Total Fat (5.7 g Mono, 2 g Poly, 3.2 g Sat); 42 mg Cholesterol; 35 g Carbohydrate; 6 g Fibre; 25 g Protein; 778 mg Sodium

Pictured on page 107.

Potluck Suggestion: Serves up to 14.

Main Dishes

Saucy Meatballs

There's enough sauce to coat a double batch of meatballs, if you need more.

Large egg, fork-beaten	1	1
Fine dry bread crumbs	1 cup	250 mL
Prepared horseradish	1 tbsp.	15 mL
Garlic clove, minced (or 1/4 tsp., 1 mL, powder)	1	1
Worcestershire sauce	1 tsp.	5 mL
Seasoned salt	1/2 tsp.	2 mL
Lean ground beef	1 lb.	454 g
BARBECUE SAUCE		
Can of crushed tomatoes	14 oz.	398 mL
Water	1 cup	250 mL
Apple cider vinegar	3/4 cup	175 mL
Chopped onion	1/2 cup	125 mL
Brown sugar, packed	1/4 cup	60 mL
Prepared mustard	2 tbsp.	30 mL
Lemon juice	1 tbsp.	15 mL
Chili powder	1 tbsp.	15 mL
Paprika	1 1/2 tsp.	7 mL
Garlic clove, minced (or 1/4 tsp., 1 mL, powder)	1	1
Cayenne pepper	1/2 tsp.	2 mL
Salt	1/2 tsp.	2 mL
Pepper	1/2 tsp.	2 mL

Combine first 6 ingredients in large bowl. Add ground beef. Mix well. Roll into 1 inch (2.5 cm) balls. Arrange in single layer in greased baking sheet with sides. Bake in 350°F (175°C) oven for about 15 minutes until no longer pink inside. Drain. Set aside.

Barbecue Sauce: Combine all 13 ingredients in large pot or Dutch oven. Bring to a boil on medium. Reduce heat to medium-low. Simmer, uncovered, for about 20 minutes, stirring occasionally, until thickened. Makes about 3 1/2 cups (875 mL) sauce. Add meatballs. Stir. Simmer, uncovered, for 25 to 30 minutes until meatballs are heated through. Serves 6.

1 serving: 326 Calories; 14.1 g Total Fat (5.8 g Mono, 1.2 g Poly, 5.2 g Sat); 78 mg Cholesterol; 32 g Carbohydrate; 2 g Fibre; 19 g Protein; 731 mg Sodium

Pictured on page 126.

Potluck Suggestion: Serves up to 10.

Chicken Sticks

A finger-licking main dish—irresistible.

HOT GARLIC SAUCE		
Cooking oil	1/2 tsp.	2 mL
Garlic clove, minced (or 1/4 tsp., 1 mL, powder)	1	1
Finely grated, peeled gingerroot (or 1/8 tsp., 0.5 mL, ground ginger)	1/2 tsp.	2 mL
Chili paste (sambal oelek)	1/8 tsp.	0.5 mL
Soy sauce	1/3 cup	75 mL
Water	1/4 cup	60 mL
Lemon juice	1 1/2 tbsp.	25 mL
Brown sugar, packed	1 1/2 tsp.	7 mL
Cornstarch	1/2 tsp.	2 mL
Can of sliced water chestnuts, drained and finely chopped	8 oz.	227 mL
Fine dry bread crumbs	1/2 cup	125 mL
Finely chopped green onion	2 tbsp.	30 mL
Soy sauce	2 tbsp.	30 mL
Finely grated, peeled gingerroot (or 1/4 tsp., 1 mL, ground ginger)	1 1/2 tsp.	7 mL
Lemon juice	1 tsp.	5 mL
Garlic clove, minced (or 1/4 tsp., 1 mL, powder)	1	1
Chili paste (sambal oelek), optional	1/4 tsp.	1 mL
Lean ground chicken	1 lb.	454 g
Bamboo skewers (8 inches, 20 cm, each), soaked in water for 10 minutes	12	12
Green leaf lettuce leaves	12	12

Hot Garlic Sauce: Heat cooking oil in small saucepan on medium. Add first amounts of garlic, ginger and chili paste. Heat and stir for 1 to 2 minutes until fragrant.

(continued on next page)

Combine next 5 ingredients in small bowl. Add to garlic mixture. Heat and stir for 3 to 4 minutes until boiling and slightly thickened. Remove from heat. Makes about 1/2 cup (125 mL) sauce. Transfer about 1/2 of sauce to separate small bowl, for basting. Set remaining sauce aside.

Combine next 8 ingredients in medium bowl. Add ground chicken. Mix well. Divide into 12 equal portions. Shape each portion into 3 inch (7.5 cm) long log.

Push 1 log lengthwise onto end of 1 skewer. Repeat with remaining logs and skewers. Place skewers crosswise on greased wire rack set in baking sheet with sides. Brush logs with basting sauce. Discard any remaining basting sauce. Broil on centre rack in oven for about 20 minutes, turning once, until logs are no longer pink inside.

Just before serving, arrange lettuce leaves on large serving platter. Arrange skewers on top of lettuce. Drizzle reserved sauce over top. Makes 12 skewers.

1 skewer: 149 Calories; 9.2 g Total Fat (2.4 g Mono, 1.2 g Poly, 0.3 g Sat); 0 mg Cholesterol; 8 g Carbohydrate; 1 g Fibre; 8 g Protein; 723 mg Sodium

———

Easy Crispy Chicken

Quick and easy. Make this the night before and chill to take to a picnic potluck.

Ranch-style dressing	1 cup	250 mL
Pepper	1 tsp.	5 mL
Bone-in chicken parts, skin removed, cut into serving size pieces	2 lbs.	900 g
Cornflake crumbs	2/3 cup	150 mL
Fine dry bread crumbs	1/3 cup	75 mL
Parsley flakes	1 tbsp.	15 mL

Combine dressing and pepper in large bowl. Add chicken. Stir until coated.

Combine remaining 3 ingredients in large resealable freezer bag. Add chicken 2 or 3 pieces at a time. Seal bag. Toss until coated. Arrange in single layer in greased baking sheet with sides. Bake in 375°F (190°C) oven for about 35 minutes until chicken is no longer pink inside. Serves 4.

1 serving: 492 Calories; 35.1 g Total Fat (1.2 g Mono, 1 g Poly, 6.2 g Sat); 96 mg Cholesterol; 17 g Carbohydrate; 1 g Fibre; 27 g Protein; 872 mg Sodium

Pictured on page 72.

Potluck Suggestion: Serves up to 8.

Chicken Empanadas

Rich, flaky pastry wraps up chicken and broccoli in a mild, cheesy sauce.
An interesting addition to a soup and sandwich potluck.
These can be made ahead and frozen.

All-purpose flour	2 1/2 cups	625 mL
Salt	1/4 tsp.	1 mL
Cold hard margarine (or butter), cut up	1 cup	250 mL
Cold water, approximately	1/4 cup	60 mL
CHEESY CHICKEN FILLING		
Diced cooked chicken	1 cup	250 mL
Block of cream cheese, softened	4 oz.	125 g
Finely chopped broccoli	1/2 cup	125 mL
Hot (or medium) salsa	1/4 cup	60 mL
Grated sharp (or medium) Cheddar cheese	1/4 cup	60 mL
Large egg, fork-beaten	1	1

Combine flour and salt in medium bowl. Cut in margarine until mixture resembles coarse crumbs. Slowly add cold water, stirring with fork until mixture starts to come together. Do not overmix. Turn out pastry onto lightly floured surface. Shape into flattened disc. Wrap with plastic wrap. Chill for 30 minutes. Discard plastic wrap. Divide pastry in half. Divide each half into 8 equal portions.

Cheesy Chicken Filling: Combine first 5 ingredients in medium bowl. Makes about 1 2/3 cups (400 mL) filling. Roll out 1 pastry portion on lightly floured surface to 4 inch (10 cm) disc. Spoon about 1 1/2 tbsp. (25 mL) filling onto centre of disc.

Lightly brush edge of pastry with egg. Fold pastry in half over filling. Pinch edges together or crimp with fork to seal. Repeat with remaining pastry portions and filling. Arrange in single layer on greased baking sheets. Brush tops and sides of empanadas with egg. Cut 1 or 2 small slits in top of each to allow steam to escape. Bake in 375°F (190°C) oven for about 25 minutes until golden. Freezes well (see Note). Makes 16 empanadas.

1 empanada: 242 Calories; 16.7 g Total Fat (9.2 g Mono, 1.6 g Poly, 4.9 g Sat); 32 mg Cholesterol; 17 g Carbohydrate; 1 g Fibre; 7 g Protein; 238 mg Sodium

Note: Freeze the baked empanadas in a single layer on waxed paper-lined baking sheets. Store in an airtight container in the freezer. Reheat in a 350°F (175°C) oven for about 15 minutes until heated through.

Potluck Suggestion: Cut each empanada in half to serve up to 32.

Cornmeal Herb Chicken

Lemon-flavoured chicken with a crunchy cornmeal crust.
Great for a harvest potluck.

SOUR CREAM MARINADE

Sour cream	1 cup	250 mL
Grated zest and juice of 1 large lemon		
Minced fresh rosemary leaves (or 3/4 tsp., 4 mL, dried, crushed)	1 tbsp.	15 mL
Chili powder	1 tbsp.	15 mL
Onion powder	1 tsp.	5 mL
Seasoned salt	1/2 tsp.	2 mL
Pepper	1/8 tsp.	0.5 mL
Boneless, skinless chicken thighs (2 – 3 oz., 57 – 85 g, each)	16	16
Yellow cornmeal	1/3 cup	75 mL
Crushed seasoned croutons	1/3 cup	75 mL
Chopped fresh parsley (or 1 1/2 tsp., 7 mL, flakes)	2 tbsp.	30 mL
Seasoned salt	1 1/2 tsp.	7 mL
Chili powder	1 tsp.	5 mL

Sour Cream Marinade: Combine first 7 ingredients in large bowl. Makes about 1 cup (250 mL) marinade.

Add chicken. Stir until coated. Cover. Marinate in refrigerator for at least 6 hours or overnight, stirring occasionally. Discard marinade.

Combine remaining 5 ingredients in small shallow dish. Press both sides of each chicken thigh into cornmeal mixture until coated. Arrange in single layer on greased foil-lined baking sheet. Spray tops of chicken thighs with cooking spray. Bake in 425°F (220°C) oven for about 20 minutes until chicken is no longer pink inside. Serves 8.

1 serving: 263 Calories; 12.2 g Total Fat (3.8 g Mono, 2 g Poly, 4.6 g Sat); 115 mg Cholesterol; 12 g Carbohydrate; 1 g Fibre; 26 g Protein; 383 mg Sodium

Potluck Suggestion: Serves up to 16.

Lemon Rosemary Chicken

Tangy, fresh-tasting lemon and rosemary sauce makes chicken an appetizing addition to any potluck.

Prepared chicken broth	1/4 cup	60 mL
Grated zest and juice of 1 large lemon		
Cornstarch	1 tbsp.	15 mL
Granulated sugar	1 tbsp.	15 mL
Chopped fresh rosemary leaves	1/2 tsp.	2 mL
Salt	1/2 tsp.	2 mL
Pepper	1/2 tsp.	2 mL
Olive (or cooking) oil	2 tbsp.	30 mL
Boneless, skinless chicken breast halves (4 – 6 oz., 113 – 170 g, each), halved crosswise	4	4
Olive (or cooking) oil	2 tbsp.	30 mL
Chopped onion	1/2 cup	125 mL
Garlic cloves, minced (or 1/2 tsp., 2 mL, powder)	2	2
Dry white (or alcohol-free) wine (or prepared chicken broth)	1/2 cup	125 mL

Combine first 7 ingredients in small bowl. Set aside.

Heat first amount of olive oil in large frying pan on medium-high. Add chicken. Cook for 1 to 2 minutes per side until browned. Transfer to large plate. Cover to keep warm.

Heat second amount of olive oil in same large frying pan. Add onion and garlic. Cook for 1 to 3 minutes, stirring often, until onion starts to soften and brown.

Add chicken and wine. Stir. Cover. Cook for 10 to 15 minutes until chicken is no longer pink inside. Stir cornstarch mixture. Add to chicken mixture. Heat and stir for about 2 minutes until sauce is boiling and thickened. Serves 4.

1 serving: 340 Calories; 16.2 g Total Fat (10.7 g Mono, 1.7 g Poly, 2.5 g Sat); 81 mg Cholesterol; 11 g Carbohydrate; 1 g Fibre; 32 g Protein; 351 mg Sodium

Potluck Suggestion: Serves up to 8.

Big Batch Barbecue Pork

Everyone will love these irresistible, saucy pork chops. Makes lots for a hungry crowd. Having a family reunion and need even more? Check out the variation!

Bone-in pork chops, trimmed of fat	25	25
Medium onions, sliced into rings	3	3
BIG BATCH BBQ SAUCE		
Tomato juice	4 cups	1 L
Finely chopped onion	1 cup	250 mL
White vinegar	1/4 cup	60 mL
Worcestershire sauce	2 tbsp.	30 mL
Brown sugar, packed	1 tbsp.	15 mL
Dry mustard	2 tsp.	10 mL
Chili powder	1 tsp.	5 mL
Salt	1 tsp.	5 mL
Pepper	1/2 tsp.	2 mL

Preheat electric grill for 5 minutes or gas barbecue to high (see Note). Cook pork chops in several batches on greased grill for about 1 minute per side until grill marks appear. Transfer to greased large roasting pan.

Layer onion rings on top of pork chops.

Big Batch BBQ Sauce: Combine all 9 ingredients in large saucepan. Bring to a boil on medium-high. Reduce heat to medium-low. Simmer, uncovered, for 15 to 20 minutes, stirring occasionally, until slightly thickened. Pour over onion. Cover. Bake in 325°F (160°C) oven for 1 1/2 to 2 hours, turning chops once, until tender. Serves 25.

1 serving: 157 Calories; 5.1 g Total Fat (2.3 g Mono, 0.6 g Poly, 1.7 g Sat); 62 mg Cholesterol; 5 g Carbohydrate; 1 g Fibre; 22 g Protein; 325 mg Sodium

Pictured on page 108.

Note: If preferred, heat a small amount of cooking oil in a large frying pan on medium-high. Cook the chops in several batches for about 1 minute per side until browned.

Variation: Omit the bone-in pork chops. Use 12 to 15 boneless pork shoulder butt steaks, halved, to make an economical batch that serves 24 to 30.

Creamy Pork And Mushrooms

*Golden pork chops are smothered with a creamy
rosemary and mushroom sauce.*

All-purpose flour	3 tbsp.	50 mL
Salt	1/4 tsp.	1 mL
Bone-in pork chops, trimmed of fat	6	6
Cooking oil	1 tbsp.	15 mL
Hard margarine (or butter)	2 tbsp.	30 mL
Sliced brown (or white) mushrooms	3 cups	750 mL
Cooking oil	1 tbsp.	15 mL
Medium leek (white part only), thinly sliced	1	1
Garlic cloves, minced (or 1 tsp., 5 mL, powder)	4	4
Dry white (or alcohol-free) wine	1 cup	250 mL
Prepared chicken broth	1 cup	250 mL
Sprigs of fresh rosemary	2	2
Salt	1/4 tsp.	1 mL
Half-and-half cream (or homogenized milk)	1/3 cup	75 mL

Measure flour and first amount of salt into large resealable freezer bag. Add 2 pork chops. Seal bag. Toss until coated. Repeat with remaining chops.

Heat first amount of cooking oil in large frying pan on medium. Cook chops in 2 batches for about 3 minutes per side until browned. Transfer to large plate. Cover to keep warm.

Melt margarine in same large frying pan on medium-high. Add mushrooms. Cook for about 5 minutes, stirring occasionally and scraping any brown bits from bottom of pan, until mushrooms are browned and liquid is evaporated. Transfer to small bowl. Cover to keep warm.

Heat second amount of cooking oil in same large frying pan on medium. Add leek and garlic. Cook for 5 to 10 minutes, stirring often, until leek is softened.

Add wine. Stir. Bring to a boil on medium-high. Boil for 3 to 5 minutes, stirring occasionally, until liquid is almost evaporated.

(continued on next page)

Main Dishes

Add broth, rosemary and second amount of salt. Stir. Add chops. Bring to a boil. Reduce heat to medium-low. Cover. Simmer for 20 minutes. Remove cover. Simmer for 15 minutes, stirring occasionally.

Add mushrooms and cream. Stir. Cook on medium for about 10 minutes, stirring occasionally, until sauce is thickened. Discard rosemary sprigs. Serves 6.

1 serving: 303 Calories; 15.3 g Total Fat (8 g Mono, 2.5 g Poly, 3.8 g Sat); 66 mg Cholesterol; 9 g Carbohydrate; 1 g Fibre; 25 g Protein; 458 mg Sodium

Pictured on page 36.

Potluck Suggestion: Up to 2 more pork chops may be added to this recipe to make extra servings.

 Provide extension cords for slow cookers or other appliances. Choose a safe area for the buffet table to keep cords from becoming a safety hazard.

Pork And Apple Skewers

Delicately spiced pork and tender-crisp apple are a great pair.

Boneless pork loin steaks, cut into 3/4 inch (2 cm) cubes	1 1/2 lbs.	680 g
SPICY ORANGE MARINADE		
Orange juice	1/3 cup	75 mL
Dry white (or alcohol-free) wine	1/4 cup	60 mL
Cooking oil	3 tbsp.	50 mL
Liquid honey	2 tbsp.	30 mL
Garlic cloves, minced (or 1/2 tsp., 2 mL, powder)	2	2
Ground cumin	1 tsp.	5 mL
Ground coriander	1/2 tsp.	2 mL
Ground cinnamon	1/2 tsp.	2 mL
Chili powder	1/4 tsp.	1 mL
Ground cloves, just a pinch		
Orange juice	1/3 cup	75 mL
Salt	1/4 tsp.	1 mL
Pepper	1/4 tsp.	1 mL
Tart medium cooking apples (such as Granny Smith), peeled, cores removed, cut into 3/4 inch (2 cm) cubes	2	2
Bamboo skewers (8 inches, 20 cm, each), soaked in water for 10 minutes	12	12

Put pork into large resealable freezer bag.

Spicy Orange Marinade: Combine first 10 ingredients in small bowl. Makes about 1 cup (250 mL) marinade. Pour over pork. Seal bag. Turn until coated. Marinate in refrigerator for at least 6 hours or overnight. Discard marinade.

Combine second amount of orange juice, salt and pepper in small bowl. Add apple. Stir gently until coated. Preheat electric grill for 5 minutes or gas barbecue to medium (see Note).

Thread pork and apple cubes alternately onto each skewer. Cook skewers on greased grill for 15 to 20 minutes, turning occasionally, until desired doneness. Makes 12 skewers.

1 skewer: 185 Calories; 11.6 g Total Fat (5.6 g Mono, 1.9 g Poly, 3 g Sat); 34 mg Cholesterol; 8 g Carbohydrate; trace Fibre; 12 g Protein; 75 mg Sodium

(continued on next page)

Main Dishes

Pictured on page 144.

Note: If preferred, place the skewers on a greased broiler pan. Broil on the centre rack in the oven for 15 to 20 minutes, turning occasionally, until desired doneness.

Glazed Baby Back Ribs

A not-too-peppery glaze coats succulent pork ribs. Add more jalapeño
pepper and extra hot pepper sauce if you prefer a spicier bite.

PEPPER GLAZE

Apple cider	2 cups	500 mL
Finely chopped red onion	1/3 cup	75 mL
Finely chopped jalapeño pepper (see Tip, page 87)	1 tbsp.	15 mL
Ketchup	1/3 cup	75 mL
Tomato paste (see Tip, page 59)	3 tbsp.	50 mL
Red wine vinegar	2 tbsp.	30 mL
Brown sugar, packed	2 tbsp.	30 mL
Hot pepper sauce	2 tbsp.	30 mL
Pepper	1/4 tsp.	1 mL
Baby back pork ribs (about 8 racks), cut into 3 – 4 bone portions	4 lbs.	1.8 kg

Pepper Glaze: Combine first 3 ingredients in medium saucepan. Bring to a boil on medium-high. Reduce heat to medium. Boil gently, uncovered, for about 15 minutes until reduced to about 1 cup (250 mL) liquid.

Add next 6 ingredients. Stir. Remove from heat. Makes about 2 cups (500 mL) glaze.

Preheat gas barbecue to medium-low. Turn off centre or left burner. Place ribs, bone-side down, on unlit side of greased grill. Brush with glaze. Close lid. Cook for 2 to 2 1/4 hours, turning ribs occasionally and brushing with glaze, until tender. Remove to large plate. Serves 8.

1 serving: 510 Calories; 35.7 g Total Fat (16.3 g Mono, 4.1 g Poly, 12.8 g Sat); 84 mg Cholesterol; 16 g Carbohydrate; 1 g Fibre; 30 g Protein; 206 mg Sodium

Pictured on page 144.

Potluck Suggestion: Serves up to 16.

Sweet And Sour Pork

Everyone will love this mildly sweet and sour combination. Chunky and colourful. Great for an Asian potluck.

All-purpose flour	1/4 cup	60 mL
Garlic salt	1 tsp.	5 mL
Paprika	1 tsp.	5 mL
Pepper	1 tsp.	5 mL
Lean boneless pork loin, cut into 1/2 inch (1.2 cm) cubes	2 lbs.	900 g
Cooking oil	2 tbsp.	30 mL
Can of stewed tomatoes (with juice), broken up	14 oz.	398 mL
Can of tomato sauce	7 1/2 oz.	213 mL
Water	1/2 cup	125 mL
White vinegar	1/3 cup	75 mL
Brown sugar, packed	1/3 cup	75 mL
Worcestershire sauce	1 tsp.	5 mL
Diced carrot	2 cups	500 mL
Sliced celery	2 cups	500 mL
Chopped onion	1 cup	250 mL
Green medium pepper, seeds and ribs removed, cut into 1 inch (2.5 cm) pieces	1	1
Red medium pepper, seeds and ribs removed, cut into 1 inch (2.5 cm) pieces	1	1
Can of sliced water chestnuts, drained	8 oz.	227 mL
Apple juice	2 tbsp.	30 mL
Cornstarch	2 tbsp.	30 mL
Soy sauce	1 tbsp.	15 mL

Combine first 4 ingredients in large resealable freezer bag. Add pork in batches. Seal bag. Toss until coated.

(continued on next page)

Main Dishes

Heat cooking oil in large frying pan on medium. Cook pork in 2 batches for about 10 minutes per batch, stirring occasionally, until browned. Transfer to ungreased 4 quart (4 L) casserole. Cover to keep warm.

Measure next 6 ingredients into same large frying pan. Heat and stir, scraping any brown bits from bottom of pan. Bring to a boil. Pour over pork.

Add carrot, celery and onion. Stir well. Cover. Bake in 350°F (175°C) oven for 1 hour. Remove from oven.

Add green and red pepper and water chestnuts. Stir.

Stir apple juice into cornstarch in small cup until smooth. Add soy sauce. Stir. Add to pork mixture. Stir well. Cover. Bake for another 30 to 45 minutes until green and red pepper are tender-crisp and sauce is boiling and slightly thickened. Serves 8.

1 serving: 345 Calories; 11.2 g Total Fat (5.4 g Mono, 2 g Poly, 2.8 g Sat); 62 mg Cholesterol; 34 g Carbohydrate; 4 g Fibre; 28 g Protein; 703 mg Sodium

Pictured on page 17.

Potluck Suggestion: Serves up to 16.

 The heat from hot peppers is in the capsaicin in the seeds and ribs. Removing the seeds and ribs will reduce the heat. Wear rubber gloves when handling hot peppers and avoid touching your eyes. Wash your hands well afterwards.

Feta Lamb Patties

Bring a little middle-eastern flavour to your next potluck. Feta cheese and a hint of lemon add a pleasant touch to these juicy lamb patties. Arrange on a bed of lettuce and garnish with lemon wedges.

Large egg, fork-beaten	1	1
Crumbled feta cheese (about 2 1/2 oz., 70 g)	1/2 cup	125 mL
Fine dry bread crumbs	1/3 cup	75 mL
Chopped fresh oregano leaves (or 1/2 tsp., 2 mL, dried)	2 tsp.	10 mL
Garlic cloves, minced (or 1/2 tsp., 2 mL, powder)	2	2
Grated lemon zest	1 tsp.	5 mL
Pepper	1/4 tsp.	1 mL
Lean ground lamb	1 lb.	454 g
Cooking oil	1 tbsp.	15 mL

Combine first 7 ingredients in large bowl. Add ground lamb. Mix well. Divide into 8 equal portions. Shape each portion into 1/2 inch (12 mm) thick patty.

Heat cooking oil in large frying pan on medium. Add patties. Cook for 3 to 4 minutes per side until no longer pink inside. Makes 8 patties.

1 patty: 183 Calories; 12.5 g Total Fat (5.1 g Mono, 1.3 g Poly, 5.1 g Sat); 74 mg Cholesterol; 4 g Carbohydrate; trace Fibre; 13 g Protein; 195 mg Sodium

Pictured on page 89.

Mediterranean Patio Potluck
1. Feta Lamb Patties, above
2. Orange Poppy Seed Cheesecake, page 130
3. Lemony Couscous Salad, page 100
4. Eggplant Onion Dip, page 20

Props courtesy of: Casa Bugatti
                      Danesco Inc.
                      Emile Henry

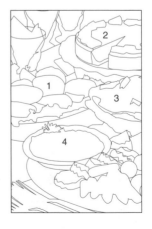

Main Dishes

Orange Almond Salad

First published in Salads, this recipe is simply delicious. Easy to double for a larger crowd and perfect for a barbecue potluck.

Head of romaine lettuce, chopped or torn	1	1
Can of mandarin orange segments, drained	10 oz.	284 mL
Slivered almonds, toasted (see Tip, page 22)	1/4 cup	60 mL
Green onions, sliced	2	2
SWEET VINAIGRETTE		
Cooking oil	1/4 cup	60 mL
White vinegar	1/4 cup	60 mL
Granulated sugar	1/4 cup	60 mL

Put first 4 ingredients into large bowl. Toss gently.

Sweet Vinaigrette: Combine cooking oil, vinegar and sugar in jar with tight-fitting lid. Shake well. Makes about 1/2 cup (125 mL) vinaigrette. Just before serving, drizzle dressing over salad. Toss gently. Makes about 10 cups (2.5 L). Serves 4.

1 serving: 268 Calories; 19.3 g Total Fat (11.5 g Mono, 5.4 g Poly, 1.5 g Sat); 0 mg Cholesterol; 23 g Carbohydrate; 3 g Fibre; 4 g Protein; 10 mg Sodium

Pictured on page 36.

Potluck Suggestion: Serves up to 10.

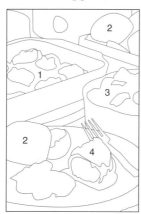

Winter Warmer Potluck
1. Blueberry Bread Pudding, page 132
2. Oatmeal Buns, page 39
3. Glazed Roasted Roots, page 111
4. Ginger Cabbage Rolls, page 68

Props courtesy of: Cherison Enterprises Inc.
Danesco Inc.
Proctor Silex® Canada
Pyrex® Portables

Dilled Potato Salad

Country-style creamy potato salad seasoned with mustard and a dash of dill.
There are no eggs in this recipe—just right for a picnic potluck.

Potatoes, peeled	2 1/2 lbs.	1.1 kg
Water		
Mayonnaise	1 cup	250 mL
Finely chopped dill pickle	2/3 cup	150 mL
Dill pickle juice	3 tbsp.	50 mL
Green onions, chopped	3	3
Prepared mustard	1 tbsp.	15 mL
Chopped fresh dill (or 1/2 tsp., 2 mL, dill weed)	2 tsp.	10 mL
Salt	1/2 tsp.	2 mL
Pepper	1/2 tsp.	2 mL
Chopped fresh parsley, for garnish	2 tsp.	10 mL

Cook potatoes in water in large pot or Dutch oven until tender. Drain. Cool. Cut potatoes into 1/2 inch (12 mm) cubes.

Combine next 8 ingredients in large bowl. Add potato. Toss gently until coated.

Garnish with parsley. Makes about 5 1/2 cups (1.4 L). Serves 6.

1 serving: 403 Calories; 31.5 g Total Fat (17.3 g Mono, 10.6 g Poly, 3 g Sat); 23 mg Cholesterol; 27 g Carbohydrate; 2 g Fibre; 4 g Protein; 710 mg Sodium

Pictured on page 72.

Potluck Suggestion: Serves up to 12.

Salads

Fruity Coleslaw

Crispy, crunchy and sweet—a pleasant change from traditional coleslaw.
A great choice for a picnic or barbecue potluck.

Shredded green cabbage, lightly packed	5 cups	1.25 L
Shredded red cabbage, lightly packed	3 cups	750 mL
Can of mandarin orange segments, drained	10 oz.	284 mL
Medium cooking apple (such as McIntosh), with peel, core removed, diced (about 1 cup, 250 mL)	1	1
ZESTY ORANGE DRESSING		
Sour cream	1 cup	250 mL
Orange juice	1/4 cup	60 mL
Liquid honey	2 tbsp.	30 mL
Grated orange zest	1/2 tsp.	2 mL
Celery seed	1/2 tsp.	2 mL
Salt	1/2 tsp.	2 mL
Pepper	1/4 tsp.	1 mL

Put first 4 ingredients into extra-large bowl. Toss.

Zesty Orange Dressing: Combine all 7 ingredients in small bowl. Makes about 1 1/3 cups (325 mL) dressing. Drizzle over salad. Toss well. Cover. Chill for at least 2 hours until cold. Remove salad with slotted spoon to large serving bowl. Discard any excess liquid. Makes about 8 cups (2 L). Serves 12.

1 serving: 70 Calories; 3.1 g Total Fat (0.9 g Mono, 0.2 g Poly, 1.8 g Sat); 8 mg Cholesterol; 11 g Carbohydrate; 1 g Fibre; 1 g Protein; 116 mg Sodium

Pictured on page 126.

Potluck Suggestion: Serves up to 18.

Paré Pointer

When the man in the moon sees that his grass is too high, "eclipse" it.

Vegetable Pecan Salad

This salad has double the crunch with crisp veggies and toasted pecans. Dresses up any potluck. If you have time, toss vegetables with vinaigrette and chill for up to 6 hours to allow flavours to blend.

Broccoli florets	2 cups	500 mL
Cauliflower florets	1 cup	250 mL
Snow peas, trimmed	4 oz.	113 g
Large red pepper, seeds and ribs removed, thinly sliced	1	1
Green onions, sliced	3	3
BALSAMIC VINAIGRETTE		
Olive (or cooking) oil	1/2 cup	125 mL
Red wine vinegar	2 tbsp.	30 mL
Balsamic vinegar	2 tbsp.	30 mL
Garlic clove, minced (or 1/4 tsp., 1 mL, powder)	1	1
Granulated sugar	1 tsp.	5 mL
Ground coriander	1 tsp.	5 mL
Salt	1/4 tsp.	1 mL
Pepper	1/4 tsp.	1 mL
Pecan halves, toasted (see Tip, page 22)	1 cup	250 mL

Put first 5 ingredients into extra-large bowl.

Balsamic Vinaigrette: Combine first 8 ingredients in small bowl. Makes about 3/4 cup (175 mL) vinaigrette. Drizzle over vegetables. Toss.

Just before serving, add pecans. Toss well. Makes about 8 cups (2 L). Serves 6.

1 serving: 332 Calories; 32.2 g Total Fat (22.1 g Mono, 4.9 g Poly, 3.6 g Sat); 0 mg Cholesterol; 11 g Carbohydrate; 3 g Fibre; 4 g Protein; 115 mg Sodium

Pictured on page 108.

Potluck Suggestion: Serves up to 12.

 Label each dish with its recipe title, noting ingredients that may be of concern for guests with dietary or allergy concerns. This is especially important for large gatherings.

Salads

Thai Slaw

Beat the blahs with bok choy. Take this interesting salad to a potluck when you feel like mixing things up a little!

THAI DRESSING

White wine vinegar	3 tbsp.	50 mL
Soy sauce	1 tbsp.	15 mL
Smooth peanut butter	1 tbsp.	15 mL
Granulated sugar	1 tsp.	5 mL
Dried crushed chilies	1/2 tsp.	2 mL
Garlic clove, minced (or 1/4 tsp., 1 mL, powder)	1	1
Water	1/2 cup	125 mL
Cornstarch	1 tsp.	5 mL
Shredded bok choy, lightly packed	3 cups	750 mL
Shredded suey choy (Chinese cabbage), lightly packed	1 cup	250 mL
Grated carrot	1 cup	250 mL
Thinly sliced red onion	1/2 cup	125 mL

Thai Dressing: Combine first 6 ingredients in small saucepan. Bring to a boil on medium.

Stir water into cornstarch in small cup until smooth. Slowly add to vinegar mixture, stirring constantly until boiling and slightly thickened. Cool. Makes about 3/4 cup (175 mL) dressing.

Put remaining 4 ingredients into large bowl. Drizzle with dressing. Toss well. Chill for at least 2 hours until cold. Makes about 8 cups (2 L). Serves 6.

1 serving: 46 Calories; 1.6 g Total Fat (0.7 g Mono, 0.5 g Poly, 0.3 g Sat); 0 mg Cholesterol; 7 g Carbohydrate; 1 g Fibre; 2 g Protein; 222 mg Sodium

Pictured on page 17.

Potluck Suggestion: Serves up to 12.

Beef And Peanut Salad

Spice up any potluck with a delicious salad. Pack the dressing, greens and peanuts in separate containers when transporting this one to the potluck. Toss just before serving so that salad greens stay crisp.

Beef top sirloin steak	1 lb.	454 g
Cooking oil	1/2 tbsp.	7 mL
Salt	1/4 tsp.	1 mL
Pepper	1/4 tsp.	1 mL
SPICY PEANUT DRESSING		
Smooth peanut butter	1/4 cup	60 mL
Plain yogurt	1/4 cup	60 mL
Chopped pickled jalapeño pepper	2 tbsp.	30 mL
Lime juice	1 tsp.	5 mL
Liquid honey	1 tsp.	5 mL
Red curry paste	3/4 tsp.	4 mL
Finely grated, peeled gingerroot (or 1/8 tsp., 0.5 mL, ground ginger)	1/2 tsp.	2 mL
Small garlic clove, minced (or 1/8 tsp., 0.5 mL, powder)	1	1
Bags of mixed salad greens (4 1/2 oz., 128 g, each)	2	2
Chopped salted peanuts (optional)	1/4 cup	60 mL

Brush both sides of steak with cooking oil. Sprinkle both sides with salt and pepper. Preheat electric grill for 5 minutes or gas barbecue to high (see Note). Cook steak on greased grill for about 5 minutes per side for medium, or until desired doneness. Cool. Cut into 1/4 inch (6 mm) strips.

Spicy Peanut Dressing: Process first 8 ingredients in blender or food processor until smooth. Makes about 2/3 cup (150 mL) dressing.

Put salad greens and beef strips into large bowl. Toss. Drizzle with dressing. Toss well.

Sprinkle with peanuts. Makes about 12 cups (3 L). Serves 6.

1 serving: 222 Calories; 14.2 g Total Fat (6.5 g Mono, 2.3 g Poly, 4.1 g Sat); 38 mg Cholesterol; 6 g Carbohydrate; 1 g Fibre; 19 g Protein; 244 mg Sodium

Pictured on page 54.

(continued on next page)

Note: If preferred, place steak on a greased broiler pan. Broil on the top rack in the oven for about 5 minutes per side until desired doneness.

Potluck Suggestion: Serves up to 10.

Foo Yong Supreme

First published in Salads, *this popular choice is definitely a classic. The dressing has a great sweet oriental flavour everyone will enjoy.*

Bacon slices, cooked crisp and crumbled	5	5
Head of romaine lettuce, chopped or torn	1	1
Fresh bean sprouts	1 cup	250 mL
Large hard-cooked eggs, finely chopped	2	2
FOO YONG DRESSING		
Cooking oil	1/4 cup	60 mL
Granulated sugar	1/4 cup	60 mL
Ketchup	3 tbsp.	50 mL
White vinegar	2 tbsp.	30 mL
Minced onion	1 tbsp.	15 mL
Worcestershire sauce	1 tsp.	5 mL

Put first 4 ingredients into large bowl. Toss.

Foo Yong Dressing: Combine all 6 ingredients in small bowl. Makes about 2/3 cup (150 mL) dressing. Just before serving, drizzle dressing over salad. Toss well. Makes about 12 cups (3 L). Serves 6.

1 serving: 202 Calories; 14.2 g Total Fat (7.6 g Mono, 3.5 g Poly, 2.2 g Sat); 76 mg Cholesterol; 14 g Carbohydrate; 1 g Fibre; 6 g Protein; 212 mg Sodium

Variation: Omit romaine lettuce. Use same amount of iceberg lettuce.

Potluck Suggestion: Serves up to 12.

Paré Pointer
Those two are always me-deep in conversation.

Japanese Cabbage Salad

This winner made its debut in Salads. *This book wouldn't be complete without this popular potluck choice. Toss with dressing just before you go to the potluck to give flavours a chance to blend.*

Medium head of cabbage, shredded	1/2	1/2
Fresh bean sprouts	4 1/2 cups	1.1 L
Sliced fresh white mushrooms	2 cups	500 mL
Sliced or slivered almonds, toasted (see Tip, page 22)	1/2 cup	125 mL
Raw sunflower seeds	1/4 cup	60 mL
Sesame seeds, toasted (see Tip, page 22)	2 tbsp.	30 mL
Green onions, chopped	2	2

ASIAN DRESSING		
Seasoning packet from instant noodles		
Cooking oil	1/2 cup	125 mL
White vinegar	3 tbsp.	50 mL
Soy sauce	2 – 4 tbsp.	30 – 60 mL
Granulated sugar	1 tbsp.	15 mL
Salt	1 tsp.	5 mL
Pepper	1/2 tsp.	2 mL
Package of instant noodles with chicken-flavoured seasoning packet	3 oz.	85 g
Dry chow mein noodles	1 1/2 cups	375 mL

Put first 7 ingredients into large bowl. Toss.

Asian Dressing: Empty seasoning packet into jar with tight-fitting lid. Add next 6 ingredients. Shake well. Makes about 3/4 cup (175 mL) dressing. Drizzle over salad. Toss well.

Just before serving, break up instant noodles. Scatter over top. Sprinkle with chow mein noodles. Makes about 20 cups (5 L). Serves 10 to 12.

1 serving: 264 Calories; 18.9 g Total Fat (9.8 g Mono, 6.4 g Poly, 1.7 g Sat); 0 mg Cholesterol; 20 g Carbohydrate; 3 g Fibre; 6 g Protein; 556 mg Sodium

Potluck Suggestion: Serves up to 20.

(continued on next page)

JAPANESE SHRIMP SALAD: Add 2 cups (500 mL) frozen cooked small shrimp (peeled and deveined), thawed, and 1/2 cup (125 mL) each of sliced English cucumber (with peel) and sliced radish to cabbage mixture before tossing.

ORIENTAL CHICKEN SALAD: Add 2 cups (500 mL) chopped cooked chicken and 1/2 cup (125 mL) each of sliced English cucumber (with peel) and sliced radish to cabbage mixture before tossing.

Mexican Salad Boats

An interesting way to present a salad at a potluck. Using romaine heart leaves makes these boats easier to pick up, but you may wish to put a large serving spoon nearby for guests to use.

Can of black beans, rinsed and drained	19 oz.	540 mL
Can of kernel corn, drained	12 oz.	341 mL
Chopped tomato	1 cup	250 mL
Chopped red onion	1/2 cup	125 mL
Chopped green pepper	1/2 cup	125 mL
Roasted red peppers, drained, blotted dry, chopped	1/2 cup	125 mL
SPICY RANCH DRESSING		
Ranch-style dressing	1/2 cup	125 mL
Ground cumin	1/2 tsp.	2 mL
Chili powder	1/2 tsp.	2 mL
Pepper	1/4 tsp.	1 mL
Romaine heart leaves	20	20

Put first 6 ingredients into medium bowl. Toss.

Spicy Ranch Dressing: Combine first 4 ingredients in small bowl. Makes about 1/2 cup (125 mL) dressing. Drizzle over bean mixture. Toss well.

Arrange lettuce leaves on large serving platter. Spoon bean mixture into each leaf. Makes 20 salad boats.

1 salad boat: 66 Calories; 3.4 g Total Fat (0 g Mono, 0.1 g Poly, 0.6 g Sat); 2 mg Cholesterol; 8 g Carbohydrate; 1 g Fibre; 2 g Protein; 133 mg Sodium

Pictured on page 107.

Lemony Couscous Salad

Vibrantly coloured with red tomato, green onion and yellow couscous.
No one will be able to resist this fresh-tasting salad.

Prepared chicken (or vegetable) broth	1 1/2 cups	375 mL
Couscous	1 1/2 cups	375 mL
Olive (or cooking) oil	1 tbsp.	15 mL
LEMON DRESSING		
Olive (or cooking) oil	3 tbsp.	50 mL
Lemon juice	3 tbsp.	50 mL
Liquid honey	1 tbsp.	15 mL
Garlic clove, minced	1	1
Salt	1/4 tsp.	1 mL
Medium tomatoes, seeds removed, chopped	3	3
Pine nuts, toasted (see Tip, page 22)	1/3 cup	75 mL
Finely chopped green onion	1/4 cup	60 mL
Fresh chili pepper, finely chopped (see Tip, page 87)	1	1
Chopped fresh mint leaves	3 tbsp.	50 mL

Measure broth into medium saucepan. Bring to a boil on medium.
Add couscous and olive oil. Stir. Cover. Remove from heat. Let stand for
5 minutes. Fluff with fork. Transfer to large bowl.

Lemon Dressing: Combine first 5 ingredients in jar with tight-fitting lid.
Shake well. Makes about 1/2 cup (125 mL) dressing. Drizzle over couscous
mixture. Toss.

Add remaining 5 ingredients. Toss well. Chill for at least 3 hours until cold.
Makes about 6 cups (1.5 L). Serves 6.

1 serving: 353 Calories; 14.8 g Total Fat (8.7 g Mono, 3.1 g Poly, 2.2 g Sat); 0 mg Cholesterol;
47 g Carbohydrate; 4 g Fibre; 11 g Protein; 316 mg Sodium

Pictured on page 89.

Potluck Suggestion: Serves up to 12.

Peach And Fennel Salad

A light, refreshing salad for a summer barbecue potluck. Use a large, fresh peach when in season, instead of canned fruit, for unbeatable flavour.

Head of romaine lettuce, chopped or torn	1	1
Can of sliced peaches in pear juice, drained and coarsely chopped	14 oz.	398 mL
Thinly sliced red onion	1/2 cup	125 mL
Fennel bulb (white part only), thinly sliced	1	1
Chopped fresh parsley	1/3 cup	75 mL
SWEET ONION DRESSING		
Olive (or cooking) oil	1 tbsp.	15 mL
Finely chopped red onion	1/3 cup	75 mL
Garlic clove, minced (or 1/4 tsp., 1 mL, powder)	1	1
Olive (or cooking) oil	3 tbsp.	50 mL
Red wine vinegar	2 tbsp.	30 mL
Maple (or maple-flavoured) syrup	1 tbsp.	15 mL
Salt	1/4 tsp.	1 mL

Put first 5 ingredients into large bowl. Toss gently.

Sweet Onion Dressing: Heat first amount of olive oil in small frying pan on medium. Add onion. Cook for 5 to 10 minutes, stirring often, until softened.

Add garlic. Heat and stir for 1 to 2 minutes until fragrant. Transfer to blender or food processor.

Add remaining 4 ingredients. Process until smooth. Makes about 1/2 cup (125 mL) dressing. Just before serving, drizzle dressing over salad. Toss gently. Makes about 13 cups (3.25 L). Serves 6.

1 serving: 154 Calories; 9.4 g Total Fat (6.8 g Mono, 0.9 g Poly, 1.3 g Sat); 0 mg Cholesterol; 17 g Carbohydrate; 2 g Fibre; 2 g Protein; 130 mg Sodium

Pictured on page 71.

Potluck Suggestion: Serves up to 12.

Italian Sausage Risotto

Great to take along to an Italian potluck.

Cooking oil	1 tsp.	5 mL
Italian sausages, casings removed, chopped	13 oz.	370 g
Chopped zucchini (with peel)	1 cup	250 mL
Chopped onion	3/4 cup	175 mL
Garlic cloves, minced (or 1/2 tsp., 2 mL, powder)	2	2
Dried basil	1/2 tsp.	2 mL
Dried whole oregano	1/2 tsp.	2 mL
Dried crushed chilies	1/2 tsp.	2 mL
Pepper	1/2 tsp.	2 mL
Arborio rice	1 1/2 cups	375 mL
Low-sodium prepared chicken broth	3 cups	750 mL
Low-sodium prepared chicken broth	1/2 cup	125 mL
Chopped tomato	1 cup	250 mL
Chopped fresh parsley (or 1 1/2 tsp., 7 mL, flakes)	2 tbsp.	30 mL
Grated Parmesan cheese	1/4 cup	60 mL

Heat cooking oil in large pot or Dutch oven on medium-high. Add sausage. Scramble-fry for about 3 minutes until starting to brown. Drain.

Add next 7 ingredients. Heat and stir for about 3 minutes until vegetables start to soften.

Add rice. Stir until coated. Add first amount of broth. Stir. Bring to a boil. Reduce heat to medium-low. Cover. Simmer for about 10 minutes, stirring once, until rice is almost tender.

Add second amount of broth. Stir. Simmer for about 15 minutes, stirring constantly, until rice is tender.

Add tomato and parsley. Stir. Remove to large serving dish.

Sprinkle with Parmesan cheese or serve cheese on the side. Serves 6.

1 serving: 340 Calories; 10.2 g Total Fat (4.5 g Mono, 1.4 g Poly, 3.7 g Sat); 26 mg Cholesterol; 47 g Carbohydrate; 1 g Fibre; 14 g Protein; 712 mg Sodium

Potluck Suggestion: Serves up to 12.

Creamy Hash Brown Bake

A tasty potato dish everyone will enjoy. This dish is a good choice when travelling some distance to a potluck as it holds its heat very well.

Hard margarine (or butter)	1 tbsp.	15 mL
Chopped onion	1/2 cup	125 mL
Can of condensed cream of chicken soup	10 oz.	284 mL
Milk	1/2 cup	125 mL
Block of cream cheese, softened and cut up	4 oz.	125 g
Dried thyme	1/4 tsp.	1 mL
Salt, just a pinch		
Pepper	1/4 tsp.	1 mL
Package of frozen hash brown potatoes, partially thawed	2 1/4 lbs.	1 kg
Grated medium Cheddar cheese	1 cup	250 mL

Melt margarine in large saucepan on medium. Add onion. Cook for 5 to 10 minutes, stirring often, until softened.

Add soup and milk. Stir. Add next 4 ingredients. Heat and stir for 3 to 4 minutes until cream cheese is melted.

Add hash brown potatoes. Stir until coated. Spread evenly in greased 2 quart (2 L) casserole. Cover. Bake in 350°F (175°C) oven for about 1 hour until edges start to brown. Remove from oven.

Sprinkle with Cheddar cheese. Bake, uncovered, for another 10 minutes until cheese is melted. Serves 6.

1 serving: 355 Calories; 19.9 g Total Fat (6.6 g Mono, 1.7 g Poly, 10.4 g Sat); 49 mg Cholesterol; 34 g Carbohydrate; 3 g Fibre; 12 g Protein; 647 mg Sodium

Potluck Suggestion: Serves up to 12.

Paré Pointer

If flying is so safe, why do airports have terminals?

Sweet Potato Casserole

This delectable dish first appeared in Vegetables *and has been a crowd-pleaser ever since. Be sure to try the variation, it tastes like dessert!*

Large eggs	2	2
Mashed sweet potato (about 2 lbs., 900 g, uncooked)	3 cups	750 mL
Granulated sugar	1/4 cup	60 mL
Hard margarine (or butter), softened	1/4 cup	60 mL
Vanilla	1 tsp.	5 mL
Salt	1/4 tsp.	1 mL
Hard margarine (or butter)	1/4 cup	60 mL
Chopped pecans	1/2 cup	125 mL
Brown sugar, packed	1/2 cup	125 mL
All-purpose flour	1/4 cup	60 mL

Combine first 6 ingredients in large bowl. Spread evenly in greased 2 quart (2 L) casserole.

Melt second amount of margarine in small saucepan. Remove from heat.

Add pecans, brown sugar and flour. Stir well. Sprinkle over potato mixture. Bake, uncovered, in 350°F (175°C) oven for about 30 minutes until heated through and golden. Serves 8.

1 serving: 331 Calories; 18.9 g Total Fat (11.7 g Mono, 2.8 g Poly, 3.4 g Sat); 54 mg Cholesterol; 38 g Carbohydrate; 2 g Fibre; 4 g Protein; 245 mg Sodium

Pictured on page 126.

Variation: Add 1/2 tsp. (2 mL) each of ground cinnamon and ground nutmeg to first 6 ingredients.

Potluck Suggestion: Serves up to 12.

Marinated Cucumbers

This pretty, summery salad with crisp vegetables and a zippy vinaigrette can be made a day ahead. Perfect for a picnic potluck.

Sliced English cucumber (with peel), about 3 medium	8 1/2 cups	2.1 L
Thinly sliced red onion	1 cup	250 mL
Roasted red peppers, drained, blotted dry, diced	1/4 cup	60 mL
GARLIC HERB VINAIGRETTE		
White vinegar	1/2 cup	125 mL
Granulated sugar	2 tbsp.	30 mL
Olive (or cooking) oil	1 1/2 tbsp.	25 mL
Dried whole oregano	1/2 tsp.	2 mL
Salt	1/2 tsp.	2 mL
Dried marjoram	1/4 tsp.	1 mL
Lemon pepper	1/4 tsp.	1 mL
Dry mustard	1/4 tsp.	1 mL
Small garlic clove, minced (or 1/8 tsp., 0.5 mL, powder)	1	1

Combine cucumber, onion and red pepper in large bowl.

Garlic Herb Vinaigrette: Measure all 9 ingredients into jar with tight-fitting lid. Shake well. Makes about 3/4 cup (175 mL) vinaigrette. Drizzle over cucumber mixture. Stir until coated. Cover. Chill for at least 6 hours or overnight. Serves 12.

1 serving: 42 Calories; 1.9 g Total Fat (1.3 g Mono, 0.2 g Poly, 0.3 g Sat); 0 mg Cholesterol; 6 g Carbohydrate; 1 g Fibre; 1 g Protein; 113 mg Sodium

Pictured on page 72.

Potluck Suggestion: Serves up to 16.

Paré Pointer
When her cat ate a ball of yarn, it had mittens.

Cheddar Salsa Cakes

Fluffy mini "pancakes" with a Tex-Mex twist. Perfect for a brunch potluck, or served with salsa and sour cream at an appetizer buffet.

Large eggs	4	4
Medium salsa	2 tbsp.	30 mL
Biscuit mix	1 cup	250 mL
Onion powder	1/4 tsp.	1 mL
Grated medium Cheddar cheese	1 cup	250 mL
Hard margarine (or butter)	1 tsp.	5 mL

Beat eggs and salsa with fork in medium bowl until well combined.

Add biscuit mix and onion powder. Stir until just moistened. Fold in cheese.

Melt margarine in large non-stick frying pan on medium-low. Drop batter, using 2 tbsp. (30 mL) for each cake, into frying pan. Cook for 1 1/2 to 2 minutes per side until puffed and golden. Makes about 12 cakes.

1 cake: 114 Calories; 6.9 g Total Fat (2.4 g Mono, 1 g Poly, 3 g Sat); 82 mg Cholesterol; 7 g Carbohydrate; trace Fibre; 5 g Protein; 228 mg Sodium

Pictured on page 107.

Fiesta Potluck
1. Chili Beef Stew, page 74
2. Pepper Cornbread Triangles, page 37
3. Cheddar Salsa Cakes, above
4. Bean-Stuffed Peppers, page 48
5. Mexican Salad Boats, page 99

Props courtesy of: Danesco Inc.
                   Island Pottery Inc.

Side Dishes

Pineapple
Upside-down

Vegetable
Pecan

Potato Puff
Casserole

Layered
Veggies and

Cheesy Baked Zucchini

Zucchini tastes so good with seasoned tomato sauce and lots of cheese.
An Italian-style, easy, bake-and-take dish.

Olive (or cooking) oil	1 tbsp.	15 mL
Garlic clove, minced (or 1/4 tsp., 1 mL, powder)	1	1
Diced zucchini (with peel)	4 cups	1 L
Tomato pasta sauce	1 3/4 cups	425 mL
Fine dry bread crumbs	1/3 cup	75 mL
Grated Parmesan cheese	3 tbsp.	50 mL
Grated part-skim mozzarella cheese	1 cup	250 mL

Combine olive oil and garlic in small cup. Brush on bottom and up sides of 2 quart (2 L) shallow baking dish.

Combine zucchini, pasta sauce and bread crumbs in large bowl. Spread evenly in prepared baking dish. Bake, uncovered, in 350°F (175°C) oven for about 40 minutes until zucchini is tender. Remove from oven.

Sprinkle Parmesan cheese over zucchini mixture. Sprinkle mozzarella cheese over top. Broil on centre rack in oven for 2 to 3 minutes until cheese is melted and golden. Serves 6.

1 serving: 216 Calories; 10.5 g Total Fat (4.9 g Mono, 1.4 g Poly, 3.6 g Sat); 14 mg Cholesterol; 23 g Carbohydrate; 3 g Fibre; 9 g Protein; 590 mg Sodium

Potluck Suggestion: Serves up to 10.

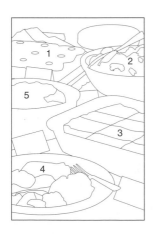

Block Party Potluck
1   Pineapple Upside-Down Cake, page 128
2. Vegetable Pecan Salad, page 94
3. Layered Veggies And Rice, page 60
4. Big Batch Barbecue Pork, page 81
5. Potato Puff Casserole, page 113

Side Dishes

Corn And Potato Scallop

Homestyle potatoes topped with golden cheese. Great for a family gathering.

Hard margarine (or butter)	1 tbsp.	15 mL
Frozen kernel corn	4 cups	1 L
Sliced fresh white mushrooms	2 cups	500 mL
Finely chopped onion	1/2 cup	125 mL
Hard margarine (or butter)	2 tbsp.	30 mL
All-purpose flour	2 tbsp.	30 mL
Milk	1 cup	250 mL
Can of condensed cream of mushroom soup	10 oz.	284 mL
Dried thyme	1/2 tsp.	2 mL
Pepper	1/2 tsp.	2 mL
Thinly sliced peeled potato	4 cups	1 L
Grated sharp Cheddar cheese	1/2 cup	125 mL
Slivered almonds, toasted (see Tip, page 22), coarsely chopped	1/4 cup	60 mL
Chopped fresh parsley, for garnish	1 tbsp.	15 mL

Melt first amount of margarine in large frying pan on medium-high. Add corn, mushrooms and onion. Cook for 5 to 10 minutes, stirring occasionally, until onion is softened and liquid is evaporated.

Add second amount of margarine. Heat and stir on medium until margarine is melted. Add flour. Heat and stir for 1 minute.

Slowly add milk, stirring constantly. Heat and stir until boiling and thickened. Add soup, thyme and pepper. Stir. Cook for about 5 minutes, stirring occasionally, until heated through. Remove from heat.

Layer 1/2 of potato slices in greased 2 quart (2 L) shallow baking dish. Spread 1/2 of corn mixture on top. Repeat with remaining potato slices and corn mixture. Bake, uncovered, in 375°F (190°C) oven for about 45 minutes until potato is tender. Remove from oven.

Combine cheese and almonds in small bowl. Sprinkle over corn mixture. Bake, uncovered, for another 10 minutes until cheese is melted.

Garnish with parsley. Serves 8.

(continued on next page)

1 serving: 302 Calories; 13.1 g Total Fat (5.9 g Mono, 2.7 g Poly, 3.8 g Sat); 9 mg Cholesterol; 41 g Carbohydrate; 4 g Fibre; 9 g Protein; 428 mg Sodium

Pictured on page 126.

Potluck Suggestion: Serves up to 16.

Glazed Roasted Roots

A vegetable medley coated with a gently sweet citrus and mustard glaze.
Put hot vegetables into a covered casserole for transporting.

Medium carrots, cut into 1 inch (2.5 cm) pieces	8	8
Parsnips, cubed	1 lb.	454 g
Potatoes, peeled and cubed	1/2 lb.	225 g
Medium onion, cut into 8 wedges	1	1
Cooking oil	3 tbsp.	50 mL
Dried thyme	1 tsp.	5 mL
Salt	1/4 tsp.	1 mL
Pepper	1/4 tsp.	1 mL
Maple (or maple-flavoured) syrup	2 tbsp.	30 mL
Dijon mustard	4 tsp.	20 mL
Frozen concentrated orange juice, thawed	1 tbsp.	15 mL

Put first 8 ingredients into large bowl. Toss until vegetables are coated. Spread evenly in greased baking sheet with sides. Bake in 400°F (205°C) oven for about 40 minutes, stirring once, until vegetables are tender.

Combine maple syrup, mustard and concentrated orange juice in same large bowl. Add vegetables. Toss until coated. Serves 6.

1 serving: 212 Calories; 7.7 g Total Fat (4.2 g Mono, 2.4 g Poly, 0.6 g Sat); 0 mg Cholesterol; 35 g Carbohydrate; 6 g Fibre; 3 g Protein; 198 mg Sodium

Pictured on page 90.

Potluck Suggestion: Serves up to 12.

Sweet Bean Pot

*A slow cooker dish that's simple to make and easy
to take to your next potluck.*

Cans of baked beans in tomato sauce (14 oz., 398 mL, each)	2	2
Can of red kidney beans, rinsed and drained	19 oz.	540 mL
Can of white kidney beans, rinsed and drained	19 oz.	540 mL
Can of pinto beans, rinsed and drained	19 oz.	540 mL
Can of lima beans, rinsed and drained	19 oz.	540 mL
Bacon slices, diced	8	8
Thinly sliced Spanish onion	1 1/2 cups	375 mL
Garlic cloves, minced (or 1/2 tsp., 2 mL, powder)	2	2
Brown sugar, packed	1 cup	250 mL
Apple cider vinegar	1/2 cup	125 mL
Dry mustard	1 tsp.	5 mL
Salt	1/2 tsp.	2 mL

Combine first 5 ingredients in 4 to 5 quart (4 to 5 L) slow cooker.
Set aside.

Cook bacon in medium frying pan on medium until almost crisp. Drain,
reserving about 2 tbsp. (30 mL) drippings in pan.

Add onion. Cook for 5 to 10 minutes, stirring often, until onion is softened
and bacon is crisp.

Add garlic. Heat and stir for 1 to 2 minutes until fragrant.

Add remaining 4 ingredients. Stir. Bring to a boil. Add to beans. Stir. Cover.
Cook on Low for 6 hours or on High for 3 hours. Serves 10.

*1 serving: 361 Calories; 6.1 g Total Fat (2.5 g Mono, 1 g Poly, 2.1 g Sat); 7 mg Cholesterol;
67 g Carbohydrate; 11 g Fibre; 14 g Protein; 924 mg Sodium*

Pictured on page 144.

Potluck Suggestion: Serves up to 20.

Potato Puff Casserole

A cheesy garlic and onion potato "soufflé." People will come back for more!

Potatoes, peeled and quartered	2 lbs.	900 g
Water		
Tub of herb and garlic spreadable cream cheese	8 oz.	250 g
2% cottage cheese	1 cup	250 mL
Hard margarine (or butter), softened	3 tbsp.	50 mL
Large eggs	2	2
Thinly sliced green onion	1/4 cup	60 mL
Salt	1 tsp.	5 mL
Pepper	1/4 tsp.	1 mL
Hard margarine (or butter)	1 tbsp.	15 mL
Fine dry bread crumbs	2 tbsp.	30 mL

Cook potato in water in large pot or Dutch oven until tender. Drain. Mash.

Beat cream cheese, cottage cheese and first amount of margarine in large bowl until well combined. Add eggs 1 at a time, beating well after each addition.

Add potato, onion, salt and pepper. Mix well. Spread evenly in greased 2 quart (2 L) casserole.

Melt second amount of margarine in small saucepan. Add bread crumbs. Stir well. Sprinkle over potato mixture. Bake, uncovered, in 325°F (160°C) oven for 30 to 35 minutes until puffed and golden. Serves 6.

1 serving: 374 Calories; 24.9 g Total Fat (10 g Mono, 1.6 g Poly, 11.8 g Sat); 121 mg Cholesterol; 25 g Carbohydrate; 2 g Fibre; 13 g Protein; 819 mg Sodium

Pictured on page 108.

Potluck Suggestion: Serves up to 12.

Paré Pointer
Farmers do a lot of whispering because the corn is all ears.

Roast Carrot Squash Soup

Smooth and gently spiced, this soup has an inviting autumn amber colour. A good choice for a Thanksgiving or Christmas potluck. Pack yogurt and cilantro separately to garnish soup at the party.

Carrots, cut into 1/2 inch (12 mm) slices	1 lb.	454 g
Acorn squash (with peel), cut into 1/2 inch (12 mm) slices	1 lb.	454 g
Chopped onion	1 cup	250 mL
Garlic cloves (with skin)	10	10
Olive (or cooking) oil	2 tbsp.	30 mL
Olive (or cooking) oil	2 tsp.	10 mL
Finely grated, peeled gingerroot (or 1/2 tsp., 2 mL, ground ginger)	2 tsp.	10 mL
Prepared chicken (or vegetable) broth	10 cups	2.5 L
Chili paste (sambal oelek)	1 tsp.	5 mL
Dried thyme	1/4 tsp.	1 mL
Ground cumin	1/4 tsp.	1 mL
Lime juice	3 tbsp.	50 mL
Grated lime zest	1 tsp.	5 mL
Pepper	1/2 tsp.	2 mL
Plain yogurt, for garnish	1/2 cup	125 mL
Chopped fresh cilantro or parsley, for garnish		

Put first 4 ingredients into large bowl. Drizzle with first amount of olive oil. Toss until coated. Spread evenly in ungreased baking sheet with sides. Bake in 425°F (220°C) oven for about 30 minutes until carrot is browned. Cool. Transfer squash and garlic to cutting board. Discard squash peels and garlic skins. Dice squash.

Heat second amount of olive oil in large pot or Dutch oven on medium. Add ginger. Heat and stir for about 1 minute until fragrant.

Add vegetables and next 4 ingredients. Stir. Bring to a boil on medium-high. Reduce heat to low. Cover. Simmer for about 20 minutes, stirring occasionally, until vegetables are tender. Remove from heat. Let stand for 10 minutes. Process soup in 4 batches in blender or food processor until smooth. Return to same large pot.

(continued on next page)

Add lime juice, zest and pepper. Stir.

Just before serving, drizzle with yogurt. Garnish with cilantro. Makes about 12 cups (3 L).

1 cup (250 mL): 98 Calories; 4.4 g Total Fat (2.8 g Mono, 0.6 g Poly, 0.8 g Sat); 0 mg Cholesterol; 10 g Carbohydrate; 2 g Fibre; 5 g Protein; 697 mg Sodium

Potluck Suggestion: Serves up to 24.

West Indies Summer Soup

Need a vacation? Invite your friends to a tacky tourist potluck to escape the winter doldrums, and serve up a taste of summer. Set the serving bowl on a bed of ice and surround it with fresh fruit slices for an inviting presentation.

Diced cantaloupe	4 cups	1 L
Diced ripe mango	2 cups	500 mL
Orange juice	2 cups	500 mL
Plain yogurt	1 cup	250 mL
Lime juice	2 tbsp.	30 mL
Liquid honey	2 tbsp.	30 mL
Ground ginger	1 tsp.	5 mL
Ground cinnamon	1/2 tsp.	2 mL

Process all 8 ingredients in blender or food processor until smooth. Transfer to large serving bowl. Chill for at least 2 hours until cold. Makes about 8 cups (2 L).

1 cup (250 mL): 126 Calories; 1 g Total Fat (0.2 g Mono, 0.1 g Poly, 0.4 g Sat); 2 mg Cholesterol; 29 g Carbohydrate; 2 g Fibre; 3 g Protein; 32 mg Sodium

Potluck Suggestion: Serves up to 16.

Paré Pointer

Benjamin Franklin discovered electricity. The real profit went to the inventor of power meters.

Broccoli And Yam Soup

"Souper" delicious—brightly coloured and bursting with flavour.
Add more curry paste if you like.

Broccoli florets	4 cups	1 L
Water		
Cooking oil	1 tbsp.	15 mL
Chopped green onion	1 cup	250 mL
Red curry paste	2 tsp.	10 mL
Garlic cloves, minced (or 1/2 tsp., 2 mL, powder)	2	2
Finely grated, peeled gingerroot (or 1/4 tsp., 1 mL, ground ginger)	1 tsp.	5 mL
Prepared chicken (or vegetable) broth	6 cups	1.5 L
Chopped peeled yam (or sweet potato)	3 cups	750 mL
Plain yogurt	1/2 cup	125 mL
Peanut butter	1/4 cup	60 mL
Salt	1/4 tsp.	1 mL

Cook broccoli in water in large pot or Dutch oven until tender. Drain. Transfer to large bowl. Set aside.

Heat cooking oil in same large pot on medium-low. Add next 4 ingredients. Stir. Cook for 5 to 10 minutes, stirring often, until onion is softened.

Add broth and yam. Stir. Bring to a boil on medium-high. Reduce heat to medium. Boil gently, uncovered, for about 20 minutes, stirring occasionally, until yam is tender. Cool slightly. Process in 3 batches in blender or food processor until smooth. Return to same large pot. Process broccoli until smooth. Add to yam mixture.

Add yogurt, peanut butter and salt. Heat and stir for about 3 minutes until heated through. Makes about 9 cups (2.25 L).

1 cup (250 mL): 179 Calories; 7.4 g Total Fat (3.5 g Mono, 2 g Poly, 1.4 g Sat); 1 mg Cholesterol; 21 g Carbohydrate; 4 g Fibre; 9 g Protein; 676 mg Sodium

Potluck Suggestion: Serves up to 18.

New England Clam Chowder

Thick and hearty, with a smoky bacon accent. Serve at a seafood buffet.

Bacon slices, diced	5	5
Chopped onion	2/3 cup	150 mL
Diced peeled potato	4 cups	1 L
Reserved liquid from clams		
Water	3/4 cup	175 mL
Cans of whole baby clams (5 oz., 142 g, each), drained and liquid reserved	2	2
Milk	3 cups	750 mL
Instant potato flakes	1 1/2 cups	375 mL
Small can of evaporated milk	5 1/2 oz.	160 mL
Seafood (or vegetable) bouillon powder	1 tbsp.	15 mL
Parsley flakes	1 tsp.	5 mL
Salt	3/4 tsp.	4 mL
Pepper	1/4 tsp.	1 mL

Cook bacon in small frying pan on medium until almost crisp. Add onion. Cook for 5 to 10 minutes, stirring often, until onion is softened and bacon is crisp.

Cook potato in clam liquid and water in large saucepan until tender.

Add bacon mixture and remaining 8 ingredients. Stir. Cook on medium for about 10 minutes, stirring occasionally, until hot but not boiling (see Note). Makes about 8 cups (2 L).

1 cup (250 mL): 228 Calories; 5.4 g Total Fat (1.9 g Mono, 0.6 g Poly, 2.5 g Sat); 29 mg Cholesterol; 31 g Carbohydrate; 2 g Fibre; 14 g Protein; 721 mg Sodium

Note: Cooking clams in boiling liquid can cause them to toughen.

Potluck Suggestion: Serves up to 16.

 Invite parents to assist children at the potluck buffet and settle them at a table before adults are served.

Tex-Mex Chowder

A light, creamy soup full of southwestern flavour. Take this to your next fiesta and serve with tortilla chips, instead of crackers.

Cooking oil	1 tsp.	5 mL
Chopped onion	1/2 cup	125 mL
Jalapeño peppers, seeds and ribs removed (see Tip, page 87), finely diced	2	2
Diced red potato (with skin)	2 cups	500 mL
Frozen kernel corn	2 cups	500 mL
Prepared chicken (or vegetable) broth	1 1/2 cups	375 mL
Ground cumin	1 tsp.	5 mL
Ground coriander	1 tsp.	5 mL
Can of skim evaporated milk	13 1/2 oz.	385 mL
Can of cream-style corn	10 oz.	284 mL
Grated Monterey Jack cheese	1/4 cup	60 mL
Salt	1/2 tsp.	2 mL
Diced tomato	1/2 cup	125 mL
Chopped fresh cilantro or parsley	1/4 cup	60 mL

Heat cooking oil in large pot or Dutch oven on medium-high. Add onion and jalapeño pepper. Cook for 5 to 10 minutes, stirring often, until onion is softened.

Add next 5 ingredients. Stir. Cover. Bring to a boil. Reduce heat to medium. Boil gently, uncovered, for about 10 minutes, stirring occasionally, until potato is tender.

Process next 4 ingredients in blender or food processor until smooth. Add to potato mixture. Heat and stir for about 3 minutes until hot but not boiling. Remove from heat.

Add tomato and cilantro. Stir. Makes about 6 3/4 cups (1.7 L).

1 cup (250 mL): 242 Calories; 8 g Total Fat (2.6 g Mono, 0.8 g Poly, 4 g Sat); 22 mg Cholesterol; 36 g Carbohydrate; 3 g Fibre; 10 g Protein; 585 mg Sodium

Potluck Suggestion: Serves up to 12.

Chunky Zucchini Soup

When there's not much time to prepare a dish for the party, get this going in the morning. Easy to take, right in the slow cooker.

Chopped zucchini (with peel)	4 cups	1 L
Chopped peeled potato	3 cups	750 mL
All-purpose flour	1/4 cup	60 mL
Prepared chicken broth	6 cups	1.5 L
Sliced leek (white part only)	3 cups	750 mL
Chopped fresh dill (or 2 1/4 tsp., 11 mL, dill weed)	3 tbsp.	50 mL
Chopped cooked ham	3 cups	750 mL
Can of evaporated milk	6 oz.	170 mL
Chopped fresh dill (or 1 1/4 tsp., 6 mL, dill weed)	1 1/2 tbsp.	25 mL

Put zucchini and potato into 4 to 5 quart (4 to 5 L) slow cooker. Add flour. Toss gently until vegetables are coated.

Add broth, leek and first amount of dill. Stir. Cover. Cook on Low for 8 to 9 hours or on High for 4 to 4 1/2 hours. Cool slightly. Transfer 3 to 4 cups (750 mL to 1 L) vegetables with slotted spoon to blender or food processor. Process until smooth. Return to slow cooker.

Add remaining 3 ingredients. Stir. Cover. Cook on High for about 15 minutes until heated through. Makes about 12 cups (3 L).

1 cup (250 mL): 172 Calories; 5.5 g Total Fat (2.3 g Mono, 0.8 g Poly, 2.1 g Sat); 26 mg Cholesterol; 16 g Carbohydrate; 2 g Fibre; 14 g Protein; 990 mg Sodium

Pictured on page 125.

Potluck Suggestion: Serves up to 24.

Paré Pointer
If money doesn't talk loud enough, turn up the volume.

Meatball Soup

A meal in a bowl. Sweet tomato broth with a dash of Parmesan cheese will have everyone returning for seconds. A great choice for an Italian potluck.

Large egg	1	1
Lean ground beef	1 lb.	454 g
Long grain white rice	1/4 cup	60 mL
Dried whole oregano	1/2 tsp.	2 mL
Cooking oil	2 tsp.	10 mL
Cooking oil	1 tsp.	5 mL
Diced carrot	1 cup	250 mL
Chopped onion	1/2 cup	125 mL
Water	2 cups	500 mL
Can of condensed tomato soup	10 oz.	284 mL
Prepared beef broth	1 cup	250 mL
Frozen peas	1/2 cup	125 mL
Grated Parmesan cheese	1/4 cup	60 mL

Beat egg with fork in large bowl. Add ground beef, rice and oregano. Mix well. Roll into 1/2 inch (1.2 cm) balls.

Heat first amount of cooking oil in large saucepan on medium. Add meatballs. Cook for about 10 minutes, turning occasionally, until browned. Transfer to paper towels to drain.

Heat second amount of cooking oil in same large saucepan on medium. Add carrot and onion. Cook for 5 to 10 minutes, stirring often, until onion is softened.

Add meatballs and next 3 ingredients. Stir. Bring to a boil on medium-high. Reduce heat to medium-low. Cover. Simmer for about 30 minutes, stirring occasionally, until meatballs are no longer pink inside and rice is tender.

Add peas and Parmesan cheese. Heat and stir for about 2 minutes until heated through. Makes about 6 cups (1.5 L).

1 cup (250 mL): 293 Calories; 16.9 g Total Fat (7.2 g Mono, 1.8 g Poly, 6 g Sat); 82 mg Cholesterol; 15 g Carbohydrate; 2 g Fibre; 20 g Protein; 663 mg Sodium

Pictured on page 125.

Potluck Suggestion: Serves up to 12.

Avocado Chicken Buns

Attractive open-face buns and tasty southwestern chicken filling make a delicious pair for your next potluck luncheon.

Boneless, skinless chicken breast halves (see Note)	1 lb.	454 g
GUACAMOLE FILLING		
Ripe medium avocados, halved	2	2
Medium salsa	1/2 cup	125 mL
Mayonnaise (not salad dressing)	1/2 cup	125 mL
Hot pepper jelly	3 tbsp.	50 mL
Finely chopped green onion	3 tbsp.	50 mL
Lemon juice	2 tsp.	10 mL
Salt	1/4 tsp.	1 mL
Deli Swiss cheese slices	8	8
Ciabatta (or kaiser) rolls, split	4	4
Halved cherry tomatoes, for garnish	1/2 cup	125 mL

Preheat electric grill for 5 minutes or gas barbecue to medium. Cook chicken breast halves on greased grill for 15 to 20 minutes, turning once, until no longer pink inside. Transfer to large plate. Cover. Chill for at least 2 hours until cold. Chop chicken.

Guacamole Filling: Mash avocado with fork in medium bowl. Add chicken and next 6 ingredients. Stir well. Makes about 4 cups (1 L) filling.

Place 1 cheese slice on each bun half. Spoon filling on top of cheese on each.

Garnish with tomato halves. Makes 8 buns.

1 bun: 568 Calories; 31.3 g Total Fat (14.4 g Mono, 6.4 g Poly, 8.3 g Sat); 77 mg Cholesterol; 41 g Carbohydrate; 3 g Fibre; 31 g Protein; 590 mg Sodium

Note: If preferred, omit the chicken breast halves and use 3 cups (750 mL) of chopped cooked chicken.

Potluck Suggestion: Cut each bun in half to serve up to 16.

Salmon Loaf Wedges

Two delicious, light fillings in one beautiful sandwich. Great for a brunch or lunch potluck. Keep loaf chilled, and slice just before serving.

SALMON FILLING

Can of red salmon, drained, skin and round bones removed	7 3/4 oz.	220 g
Mayonnaise	1/4 cup	60 mL
Minced onion flakes (or 1 tbsp., 15 mL, thinly sliced green onion)	1/2 tsp.	2 mL
Parsley flakes	1/2 tsp.	2 mL
Salt	1/8 tsp.	0.5 mL

EGG FILLING

Large hard-cooked eggs, chopped	4	4
Mayonnaise	1/4 cup	60 mL
Finely diced celery	1 1/2 tbsp.	25 mL
Dried chives	1/2 tsp.	2 mL
Onion powder	1/4 tsp.	1 mL
Salt	1/4 tsp.	1 mL

Round bread loaf (such as pumpernickel, rye or sourdough), about 8 inch (20 cm) diameter	1	1
Hard margarine (or butter), softened (optional)	2 tbsp.	30 mL

Salmon Filling: Combine all 5 ingredients in small bowl. Makes about 3/4 cup (175 mL) filling.

Egg Filling: Combine first 6 ingredients in small bowl. Makes about 1 cup (250 mL) filling.

Slice bread loaf horizontally into 3 equal layers. Place bottom layer, cut-side up, on cutting board. Spread 1 tbsp. (15 mL) margarine on cut-side. Spread Salmon Filling over margarine. Place centre layer of loaf on top of filling. Spread remaining margarine on top. Spread Egg Filling over margarine. Cover with top layer of loaf. Press down lightly. Cuts into 8 wedges.

1 wedge: 337 Calories; 18.9 g Total Fat (9.4 g Mono, 5.5 g Poly, 2.9 g Sat); 123 mg Cholesterol; 28 g Carbohydrate; 4 g Fibre; 13 g Protein; 629 mg Sodium

Pictured on page 125.

Potluck Suggestion: Cut into 12 wedges.

Pepper Beef Pinwheels

Colourful spinach and red pepper make these an especially attractive addition to any potluck. Take wrapped and chilled rolls in a cooler to the potluck and slice just before serving.

Tub of herb and garlic spreadable cream cheese	8 oz.	250 g
Flour tortillas (9 inch, 22 cm, diameter)	8	8
Thinly sliced deli roast beef	1 1/2 lbs.	680 g
Fresh spinach, stems removed, lightly packed	4 cups	1 L
Roasted red peppers, drained, blotted dry, cut into strips	2 1/2 cups	625 mL

Spread cream cheese evenly on 1 side of each tortilla, almost to edge.

Layer roast beef on top of cream cheese, leaving 1/2 inch (12 mm) edge. Layer spinach over beef.

Layer red pepper strips across each tortilla, about 2 inches (5 cm) from edge. Roll up tightly, jelly roll-style. Trim ends. Cut each roll diagonally, sushi-style (see Diagram), into 8 equal slices (see Note). Makes 64 slices.

1 slice: 51 Calories; 2.3 g Total Fat (0.8 g Mono, 0.2 g Poly, 1.1 g Sat); 11 mg Cholesterol; 4 g Carbohydrate; trace Fibre; 4 g Protein; 47 mg Sodium

Pictured on front cover.

Note: For best results, wrap each roll with plastic wrap and chill overnight before cutting.

PEPPER ARUGULA PINWHEELS: Omit spinach. Use same amount of arugula.

SPINACH SALAMI PINWHEELS: Omit roast beef. Use same amount of Genoa or Cervelat salami.

Seafood Croissants

Petite croissants stuffed with a lovely citrus-flavoured seafood salad
are an elegant addition to a light luncheon potluck.

SHRIMP FILLING

Frozen cooked baby shrimp, thawed, drained, blotted dry	3/4 lb.	340 g
Diced Monterey Jack With Jalapeño cheese	2/3 cup	150 mL
Diced English cucumber (with peel)	2/3 cup	150 mL
Can of crabmeat, drained, cartilage removed (or imitation), flaked	5 oz.	142 g
Mayonnaise	1/2 cup	125 mL
Lemon juice	2 tsp.	10 mL
Seafood cocktail sauce	3/4 cup	175 mL
Mini croissants, split	18	18
Butter lettuce leaves, halved	9	9

Shrimp Filling: Combine first 6 ingredients in medium bowl. Makes about 3 1/2 cups (875 mL) filling.

Spread about 2 tsp. (10 mL) cocktail sauce on top half of each croissant. Spoon about 3 tbsp. (50 mL) filling onto each bottom half.

Place 1 lettuce leaf half on top of filling on each. Cover with top halves of croissants. Makes 18 croissants.

1 croissant: 238 Calories; 14.2 g Total Fat (5.8 g Mono, 2.3 g Poly, 5.5 g Sat); 70 mg Cholesterol; 18 g Carbohydrate; 1 g Fibre; 9 g Protein; 537 mg Sodium

Pictured on page 125.

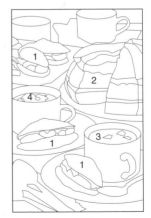

Soup & Sandwich Potluck
1. Seafood Croissants, above
2. Salmon Loaf Wedges, page 122
3. Chunky Zucchini Soup, page 119
4. Meatball Soup, page 120

BBQ Beef Bunwiches

Sweet, tangy, shredded beef cooked to tender perfection in a slow cooker.
A hearty sandwich for a soup and sandwich potluck.

Boneless blade (or chuck) roast	3 lbs.	1.4 kg
Apple cider vinegar	3/4 cup	175 mL
Ketchup	3/4 cup	175 mL
Brown sugar, packed	3 tbsp.	50 mL
Dijon mustard	1 tbsp.	15 mL
Salt	1/2 tsp.	2 mL
Dried crushed chilies	1/4 tsp.	1 mL
Hamburger buns, split and toasted	12	12

Place roast in 4 to 5 quart (4 to 5 L) slow cooker.

Combine next 6 ingredients in medium bowl. Pour over roast. Turn roast until coated. Cover. Cook on Low for 8 hours or on High for 4 hours. Transfer roast to large plate. Transfer sauce to heatproof 4 cup (1 L) liquid measure. Shred beef with 2 forks. Return beef to slow cooker. Skim any fat from surface of sauce. Add sauce to beef. Stir well.

Spoon beef mixture onto bottom half of each bun. Cover with top halves. Makes 12 bunwiches.

1 bunwich: 262 Calories; 7.5 g Total Fat (3.3 g Mono, 0.6 g Poly, 2.5 g Sat); 38 mg Cholesterol; 30 g Carbohydrate; 1 g Fibre; 18 g Protein; 572 mg Sodium

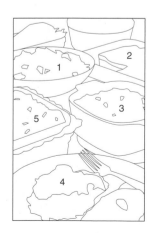

Family Reunion Potluck
1. Fruity Coleslaw, page 93
2. Banana Trifle Squares, page 140
3. Sweet Potato Casserole, page 104
4. Saucy Meatballs, page 75
5. Corn And Potato Scallop, page 110

Props courtesy of: Pfaltzgraff Canada
Pyrex® Bakeware

Pineapple Upside-Down Cake

A sweet, moist cake with pineapple slices and a cherry sitting pretty on each slice. Take whipped cream in a separate container to the potluck for guests to spoon over top.

Brown sugar, packed	1/2 cup	125 mL
Hard margarine (or butter)	1/4 cup	60 mL
Can of pineapple slices, drained	14 oz.	398 mL
Red glazed cherries, approximately	9	9
Hard margarine (or butter), softened	1/3 cup	75 mL
Granulated sugar	3/4 cup	175 mL
Large egg	1	1
Vanilla	1/2 tsp.	2 mL
All-purpose flour	2 cups	500 mL
Baking powder	4 tsp.	20 mL
Salt	1/2 tsp.	2 mL
Milk	2/3 cup	150 mL

Heat and stir brown sugar and first amount of margarine in small saucepan on medium for about 4 minutes until brown sugar is dissolved. Spread evenly in greased waxed paper-lined 9 x 9 inch (22 x 22 cm) pan.

Arrange pineapple slices in single layer on top of brown sugar mixture. Place 1 cherry in centre of each slice.

Cream second amount of margarine and granulated sugar in medium bowl. Add egg. Beat well. Add vanilla. Beat until smooth.

Combine flour, baking powder and salt in small bowl. Add to margarine mixture in 3 additions, alternating with milk in 2 additions, beginning and ending with flour mixture, beating well after each addition. Carefully pour over pineapple slices. Spread evenly. Bake in 350°F (175°C) oven for 35 to 40 minutes until wooden pick inserted in centre comes out clean. Let stand in pan on wire rack for 5 minutes. Invert onto large serving plate. Discard waxed paper. Cuts into 9 pieces.

1 piece: 391 Calories; 13.6 g Total Fat (8.5 g Mono, 1.5 g Poly, 2.9 g Sat); 25 mg Cholesterol; 64 g Carbohydrate; 1 g Fibre; 5 g Protein; 466 mg Sodium

Pictured on page 108.

Potluck Suggestion: Cut into 18 pieces.

Creamy Peanut Butter Pie

Chocolate and peanut butter make a great pair in this chilled pie that kids of all ages will love. Certain to become a potluck favourite.

CHOCOLATE PEANUT CRUST

Hard margarine (or butter)	1/3 cup	75 mL
Chocolate wafer crumbs	2 cups	500 mL
Crunchy peanut butter	1/4 cup	60 mL
Icing (confectioner's) sugar	1 tbsp.	15 mL
Granulated sugar	2/3 cup	150 mL
Cornstarch	3 tbsp.	50 mL
All-purpose flour	3 tbsp.	50 mL
Salt	1/2 tsp.	2 mL
Large eggs, fork-beaten	2	2
Milk	3 cups	750 mL
Hard margarine (or butter)	2 tbsp.	30 mL
Crunchy peanut butter	1/4 cup	60 mL
Vanilla	1 tsp.	5 mL
Frozen whipped topping, thawed	2 cups	500 mL

Chocolate Peanut Crust: Melt first amount of margarine in small saucepan. Remove from heat. Add wafer crumbs, first amount of peanut butter and icing sugar. Mix well. Reserve 3 tbsp. (50 mL) crumb mixture in small cup. Press remaining crumb mixture firmly in bottom and up side of ungreased 9 inch (22 cm) deep dish pie plate. Bake in 350°F (175°C) oven for 10 minutes. Cool.

Combine next 4 ingredients in large saucepan.

Add egg, milk and second amount of margarine. Stir. Bring to a boil on medium, stirring constantly for 2 minutes. Remove from heat.

Add second amount of peanut butter and vanilla. Stir well. Spread evenly in cooled crust. Chill for at least 2 hours until set.

Spread whipped topping on top of pie. Sprinkle with reserved crumbs. Cuts into 8 wedges.

1 wedge: 545 Calories; 31 g Total Fat (14.5 g Mono, 4.4 g Poly, 10.3 g Sat); 58 mg Cholesterol; 58 g Carbohydrate; 1 g Fibre; 12 g Protein; 601 mg Sodium

Pictured on page 143.

Potluck Suggestion: Cut into 12 wedges.

Orange Poppy Seed Cheesecake

This pretty cheesecake, speckled with poppy seeds, is sure to stand out on any potluck dessert table. Refreshing citrus flavour provides a nice ending to a delicious meal shared with friends.

Hard margarine (or butter)	1/2 cup	125 mL
Graham cracker crumbs	2 cups	500 mL
Envelopes of unflavoured gelatin (1/4 oz., 7 g, each)	2	2
Water	1/3 cup	75 mL
Blocks of cream cheese (8 oz., 250 g, each), softened	2	2
Plain yogurt	1 cup	250 mL
Granulated sugar	3/4 cup	175 mL
Orange juice	1/4 cup	60 mL
Grated orange zest	2 tbsp.	30 mL
Poppy seeds	3 tbsp.	50 mL
ORANGE TOPPING		
Orange juice	3/4 cup	175 mL
Cornstarch	1 1/2 tbsp.	25 mL
Granulated sugar	1 tbsp.	15 mL
Orange-flavoured liqueur (such as Grand Marnier), optional	1 tbsp.	15 mL
Whipped cream, for garnish		
Orange slices, for garnish		

Melt margarine in small saucepan. Remove from heat. Add graham crumbs. Mix well. Press firmly in bottom and up side of ungreased 9 inch (22 cm) springform pan. Chill for 1 hour.

Sprinkle gelatin over water in separate small saucepan. Let stand for 1 minute. Heat and stir on low for 1 to 2 minutes until gelatin is dissolved.

Beat next 5 ingredients in large bowl until well combined.

Add gelatin mixture and poppy seeds. Beat until smooth. Spread evenly in crust. Cover. Chill for at least 3 hours until set.

(continued on next page)

Desserts

Orange Topping: Combine first 3 ingredients in medium saucepan. Heat and stir on medium-high for 3 to 4 minutes until boiling and thickened. Remove from heat.

Add liqueur. Stir. Let stand for 10 minutes. Spread evenly on top of cheesecake. Chill for at least 1 hour until set. Run knife around inside edge of pan to loosen cheesecake before removing side of pan.

Garnish with whipped cream and orange slices. Cuts into 12 wedges.

1 wedge: 379 Calories; 25.5 g Total Fat (10.3 g Mono, 2.3 g Poly, 11.5 g Sat); 47 mg Cholesterol; 32 g Carbohydrate; 1 g Fibre; 7 g Protein; 325 mg Sodium

Pictured on page 89.

Potluck Suggestion: Cut into 20 wedges.

 Ensure each dish has a separate serving spoon. When items are accessible from both sides of the buffet table, place two serving spoons in each dish so guests can reach them from either side.

Blueberry Bread Pudding

Tasty blueberry sauce with a subtle orange accent crowns baguette slices baked in a creamy custard. Just right for a winter potluck.

Hard margarine (or butter), softened	3 tbsp.	50 mL
Baguette bread loaf, cut into 12 slices	1	1
Half-and-half cream (or homogenized milk)	3 cups	750 mL
Large eggs	5	5
Granulated sugar	1/2 cup	125 mL
Vanilla	2 tbsp.	30 mL
BLUEBERRY SAUCE		
Fresh (or frozen) blueberries	2 cups	500 mL
Blueberry jam	1/4 cup	60 mL
Orange-flavoured liqueur (such as Grand Marnier)	3 tbsp.	50 mL
Granulated sugar	2 tbsp.	30 mL
Water	2 tbsp.	30 mL

Spread margarine on 1 side of each bread slice. Arrange slices, margarine-side up, in single layer in greased 3 quart (3 L) shallow baking dish.

Heat cream in medium saucepan on medium for about 8 minutes until bubbles start to form around edge.

Beat eggs, sugar and vanilla in large bowl until thick and pale. Slowly add 1/2 cup (125 mL) warmed cream, stirring constantly. Slowly add remaining cream, stirring constantly until well combined. Pour evenly over bread slices. Place baking dish in large roasting pan. Carefully pour boiling water into pan until halfway up side of baking dish. Bake, uncovered, in 350°F (175°C) oven for about 35 minutes until just set. Carefully remove baking dish from roasting pan. Let stand for 15 minutes.

Blueberry Sauce: Combine all 5 ingredients in medium frying pan. Bring to a boil on medium-high, stirring constantly. Boil for about 3 minutes, without stirring, until slightly thickened. Makes about 1 cup (250 mL) sauce. Spoon over each bread slice in baking dish. Serves 12.

1 serving: 272 Calories; 12.1 g Total Fat (4.8 g Mono, 0.9 g Poly, 5.3 g Sat); 110 mg Cholesterol; 32 g Carbohydrate; 1 g Fibre; 6 g Protein; 206 mg Sodium

Pictured on page 90.

Potluck Suggestion: Serves up to 24.

Pear Flower Gingerbread

Mellow fruit flavour "pears up" with traditional gingerbread spices in this attractive upside-down cake.

Hard margarine (or butter)	1/4 cup	60 mL
Brown sugar, packed	1/4 cup	60 mL
Large fresh pear, peeled, core removed, cut into 1/4 inch (6 mm) slices	1	1
Large egg	1	1
Milk	1/2 cup	125 mL
Fancy (mild) molasses	1/2 cup	125 mL
Cooking oil	1/4 cup	60 mL
Whole wheat flour	1 1/2 cups	375 mL
Brown sugar, packed	1/2 cup	125 mL
Ground ginger	1 tsp.	5 mL
Ground cinnamon	1 tsp.	5 mL
Ground cloves	1/2 tsp.	2 mL
Ground nutmeg	1/2 tsp.	2 mL
Baking soda	1/2 tsp.	2 mL
Salt	1/4 tsp.	1 mL

Heat and stir margarine and first amount of brown sugar in small saucepan on medium for 3 to 4 minutes until brown sugar is dissolved. Spread evenly in greased 9 inch (22 cm) round pan.

Arrange pear slices in flower pattern on top of brown sugar mixture.

Beat egg and milk in large bowl until frothy. Add molasses and cooking oil. Beat until smooth.

Combine remaining 8 ingredients in medium bowl. Add to egg mixture. Stir until just moistened. Carefully pour batter over pear slices. Spread evenly. Bake in 350°F (175°C) oven for about 40 minutes until wooden pick inserted in centre comes out clean. Let stand in pan for 10 minutes. Invert onto large serving plate. Cuts into 8 wedges.

1 wedge: 369 Calories; 14.7 g Total Fat (8.6 g Mono, 3 g Poly, 2.2 g Sat); 28 mg Cholesterol; 58 g Carbohydrate; 4 g Fibre; 5 g Protein; 261 mg Sodium

Pictured on page 71.

Potluck Suggestion: Cut into 12 wedges.

Chocolate Raspberry Flan

Luscious raspberries and silky almond custard rest on a tasty chocolate crust.
Potluck guests will think it's simply flan-tastic!

CHOCOLATE CRUST

All-purpose flour	1 1/2 cups	375 mL
Granulated sugar	1/4 cup	60 mL
Cocoa, sifted if lumpy	2 tbsp.	30 mL
Cold hard margarine (or butter), cut up	1/2 cup	125 mL
Water	1/4 cup	60 mL

ALMOND CUSTARD

Egg yolks (large)	2	2
Homogenized milk	1 1/4 cups	300 mL
Granulated sugar	1/2 cup	125 mL
All-purpose flour	2 1/2 tbsp.	37 mL
Cornstarch	2 tbsp.	30 mL
Salt	1/8 tsp.	0.5 mL
Hard margarine (or butter)	2 tsp.	10 mL
Almond flavouring	1/2 tsp.	2 mL
Semi-sweet chocolate baking squares (1 oz., 28 g, each), chopped	2	2
Fresh raspberries	2 – 3 cups	500 – 750 mL

Chocolate Crust: Combine first 3 ingredients in medium bowl. Cut in margarine until mixture resembles coarse crumbs. Slowly add water 1 tbsp. (15 mL) at a time, stirring with fork until mixture starts to come together. Do not overmix. Turn out pastry onto lightly floured surface. Shape into flattened disc. Wrap with plastic wrap. Chill for 30 minutes. Discard plastic wrap. Roll out pastry on lightly floured surface to fit greased 9 inch (22 cm) tart pan with fluted sides and removable bottom. Carefully lift pastry and press in bottom and up side of pan. Trim edge. Chill for 30 minutes. Place pan on ungreased baking sheet (see Note). Cover pastry with parchment paper, extending paper over side of pan. Fill pan halfway with dried beans. Bake in 350°F (175°C) oven for about 25 minutes until crust on side is firm. Remove from oven. Carefully remove parchment paper and beans, reserving beans for next time you bake pastry. Bake for another 10 minutes until bottom is firm. Let stand on baking sheet on wire rack until cooled completely.

(continued on next page)

Almond Custard: Combine first 6 ingredients in small saucepan. Heat and stir on medium for about 7 minutes until boiling and thickened. Remove from heat.

Add margarine and flavouring. Stir until margarine is melted. Transfer to small heatproof bowl. Cover with plastic wrap directly on surface to prevent skin from forming. Cool to room temperature.

Heat chocolate in small heavy saucepan on lowest heat, stirring often until almost melted. Do not overheat. Remove from heat. Stir until smooth. Spread evenly on bottom and side of crust. Let stand for about 15 minutes until set. Spread custard on top of chocolate.

Arrange raspberries, stem-end down, in single layer on top of custard. Chill for at least 1 hour until custard is set. Cuts into 8 wedges.

1 wedge: 392 Calories; 18.4 g Total Fat (10.2 g Mono, 1.8 g Poly, 5.3 g Sat); 59 mg Cholesterol; 53 g Carbohydrate; 3 g Fibre; 6 g Protein; 215 mg Sodium

Pictured on page 54.

Note: Placing the tart pan on a baking sheet provides a safe way to remove the hot pan from the oven.

Potluck Suggestion: Cut into 12 wedges.

Paré Pointer

There are many know-it-all kids living with their no-it-all parents.

Bumbleberry Streusel Cake

This colourful coffee cake is ideal for an office potluck.

All-purpose flour	1 2/3 cups	400 mL
Granulated sugar	1 cup	250 mL
Baking powder	1 tbsp.	15 mL
Salt	1/2 tsp.	2 mL
Ground cinnamon	1/4 tsp.	1 mL
Cold hard margarine (or butter), cut up	1/3 cup	75 mL
Large egg, fork-beaten	1	1
Milk	1/2 cup	125 mL
Grated orange zest	2 tsp.	10 mL
Vanilla	1/2 tsp.	2 mL
Fresh (or frozen) blueberries	1 cup	250 mL
Fresh (or frozen) raspberries	1 cup	250 mL
Chopped fresh (or frozen) rhubarb	1 cup	250 mL
ALMOND STREUSEL TOPPING		
All-purpose flour	1 cup	250 mL
Brown sugar, packed	1/2 cup	125 mL
Ground cinnamon	1/4 tsp.	1 mL
Cold hard margarine (or butter), cut up	1/2 cup	125 mL
Sliced almonds	1 cup	250 mL

Combine first 5 ingredients in large bowl. Cut in margarine until mixture resembles coarse crumbs. Make a well in centre.

Add next 4 ingredients to well. Stir until just moistened. Spread evenly in greased 9 x 13 inch (22 x 33 cm) pan.

Scatter blueberries, raspberries and rhubarb over batter.

Almond Streusel Topping: Combine first 3 ingredients in medium bowl. Cut in margarine until mixture resembles fine crumbs. Add almonds. Stir. Makes about 2 1/2 cups (625 mL) topping. Sprinkle over fruit. Bake in 350°F (175°C) oven for about 55 minutes until golden and wooden pick inserted in centre comes out clean. Let stand for 10 minutes. Cuts into 15 pieces.

1 piece: 329 Calories; 15.4 g Total Fat (9.7 g Mono, 2 g Poly, 2.8 g Sat); 15 mg Cholesterol; 45 g Carbohydrate; 2 g Fibre; 5 g Protein; 293 mg Sodium

Pictured on page 35.

Potluck Suggestion: Cut into 20 pieces.

Praline Cheesecake Tarts

Caramel-coated pecans and a drizzle of chocolate top a rich cheesecake filling.
An elegant presentation to take to a potluck where the "wow" factor counts.

Tart shells (3 inch, 7.5 cm, size)	24	24
CHEESECAKE FILLING		
Block of cream cheese, softened	8 oz.	250 g
Sour cream	1 cup	250 mL
Granulated sugar	3/4 cup	175 mL
All-purpose flour	2 tbsp.	30 mL
Large eggs	2	2
Vanilla	1 tsp.	5 mL
PRALINE		
Caramel (or butterscotch) ice cream topping	1/2 cup	125 mL
Finely chopped pecans, toasted (see Tip, page 22)	1/2 cup	125 mL
Semi-sweet chocolate chips	1/2 cup	125 mL
Hard margarine (or butter)	2 tbsp.	30 mL

Place tart shells on ungreased baking sheets. Bake in 350°F (175°C) oven for about 10 minutes until edges are just golden. Cool.

Cheesecake Filling: Beat first 4 ingredients in large bowl until smooth.

Add eggs 1 at a time, beating after each addition until just combined. Add vanilla. Stir. Makes about 3 1/2 cups (875 mL) filling. Spoon into tart shells. Spread evenly. Bake for about 20 minutes until set. Cool.

Praline: Combine ice cream topping and pecans in small bowl. Makes about 2/3 cup (150 mL). Spoon over filling.

Heat chocolate chips and margarine in small heavy saucepan on lowest heat, stirring often until almost melted. Do not overheat. Remove from heat. Stir until smooth. Spoon into pastry bag fitted with small writing tip or small resealable freezer bag with tiny piece snipped off corner. Drizzle chocolate in decorative pattern over praline on each. Makes 24 tarts.

1 tart: 212 Calories; 13.4 g Total Fat (5.6 g Mono, 1.3 g Poly, 5.6 g Sat); 33 mg Cholesterol;
22 g Carbohydrate; trace Fibre; 3 g Protein; 158 mg Sodium

Pictured on page 143.

Ginger Pear Cheesecake

Gingery cheese filling rests on a shortbread crust, all topped with glistening pear slices. An easy-to-make, attractive dessert that's perfect when you want to take something a bit fancier.

ALMOND SHORTBREAD CRUST		
Hard margarine (or butter)	1/3 cup	75 mL
Shortbread cookie crumbs	1 1/2 cups	375 mL
Ground almonds	1/2 cup	125 mL
Cans of pear halves in light syrup (14 oz., 398 mL, each), drained and syrup reserved	2	2
Envelope of unflavoured gelatin	1/4 oz.	7 g
Reserved pear syrup	1/3 cup	75 mL
Blocks of cream cheese (8 oz., 250 g, each), softened	2	2
Sour cream	1 cup	250 mL
Brown sugar, packed	3/4 cup	175 mL
Minced crystallized ginger	1/4 cup	60 mL
Grated lemon zest	1/2 tsp.	2 mL
Ground cinnamon	1/4 tsp.	1 mL
Ground nutmeg	1/4 tsp.	1 mL
MAPLE PEAR TOPPING		
Unflavoured gelatin	1 tsp.	5 mL
Reserved pear syrup	1/3 cup	75 mL
Maple (or maple-flavoured) syrup	1/4 cup	60 mL
Lemon juice	1 tsp.	5 mL

Almond Shortbread Crust: Melt margarine in medium saucepan. Remove from heat. Add cookie crumbs and almonds. Mix well. Press firmly in bottom of greased 10 inch (25 cm) springform pan. Bake in 350°F (175°C) oven for 10 minutes. Cool.

Blot pears dry with paper towels. Slice thinly. Set aside.

Sprinkle gelatin over reserved pear syrup in small saucepan. Let stand for 1 minute. Heat and stir on low for 1 to 2 minutes until gelatin is dissolved.

(continued on next page)

138   Desserts

Beat next 7 ingredients in large bowl until well combined. Add gelatin mixture. Beat until smooth. Spread evenly on crust. Arrange pear slices in decorative pattern on top of cream cheese mixture. Cover. Chill for at least 3 hours until set.

Maple Pear Topping: Sprinkle gelatin over reserved pear syrup in small saucepan. Let stand for 1 minute. Heat and stir on low for 1 to 2 minutes until gelatin is dissolved.

Add maple syrup and lemon juice. Stir. Cool to room temperature. Carefully spoon over pear slices, allowing gelatin mixture to pool between slices. Chill for at least 1 hour until set. Run knife around inside edge of pan to loosen cheesecake before removing side of pan. Cuts into 12 wedges.

1 wedge: 401 Calories; 25.9 g Total Fat (10.3 g Mono, 1.7 g Poly, 12.6 g Sat); 55 mg Cholesterol; 39 g Carbohydrate; 1 g Fibre; 6 g Protein; 239 mg Sodium

Pictured on page 36.

Potluck Suggestion: Cut into 24 wedges.

When providing beverages, ensure alcohol-free choices are available. Fill pitchers with ice water, and make coffee and tea. If children are invited, protect your carpet and your guests' feelings by avoiding deeply coloured punches.

Banana Trifle Squares

An easy dessert that's destined to become popular potluck fare.

FIRST LAYER		
Hard margarine (or butter)	1/2 cup	125 mL
Graham cracker crumbs	2 cups	500 mL
Granulated sugar	2 tbsp.	30 mL
SECOND LAYER		
Box of instant vanilla pudding powder (4 serving size)	1	1
Milk	1 1/2 cups	375 mL
Medium bananas, sliced	4	4
THIRD LAYER		
Box of instant butterscotch pudding powder (4 serving size)	1	1
Milk	1 1/2 cups	375 mL
FOURTH LAYER		
Envelopes of dessert topping (not prepared)	2	2
Milk	2/3 cup	150 mL

First Layer: Melt margarine in medium saucepan. Remove from heat. Add graham crumbs and sugar. Mix well. Reserve 3 tbsp. (50 mL) crumb mixture in small cup. Press remaining crumb mixture firmly in bottom of ungreased 9 x 13 inch (22 x 33 cm) pan.

Second Layer: Beat vanilla pudding powder and milk in small bowl until smooth and starting to thicken. Spread evenly on top of first layer. Arrange banana slices on top of pudding.

Third Layer: Beat butterscotch pudding powder and milk in separate small bowl until smooth and starting to thicken. Spread evenly on top of banana.

Fourth Layer: Beat dessert topping and milk in medium bowl until stiff peaks form. Spread evenly on top of third layer. Sprinkle with reserved crumb mixture. Chill. Cuts into 15 pieces.

1 piece: 253 Calories; 10.9 g Total Fat (5.1 g Mono, 0.9 g Poly, 4.2 g Sat); 3 mg Cholesterol; 37 g Carbohydrate; 1 g Fibre; 4 g Protein; 391 mg Sodium

Pictured on page 126.

Potluck Suggestion: Cut into 24 pieces.

Grilled Pineapple Chunks

When the barbecue potluck is at your house, serve these sumptuous chunks of grilled pineapple for dessert. A fluffy orange sauce adds interest to these sweet and tangy treats.

Maple (or maple-flavoured) syrup	1/4 cup	60 mL
Hard margarine (or butter)	3 tbsp.	50 mL
Granulated sugar	3 tbsp.	50 mL
Orange-flavoured liqueur (such as Grand Marnier)	3 tbsp.	50 mL
Ground nutmeg	1/2 tsp.	2 mL
Large fresh pineapple, quartered lengthwise, core removed	1	1
ORANGE MASCARPONE SAUCE		
Package of mascarpone cheese, softened	8 oz.	250 g
Icing (confectioner's) sugar	2 tbsp.	30 mL
Orange-flavoured liqueur (such as Grand Marnier)	2 tbsp.	30 mL
Grated orange zest	1/2 tsp.	2 mL

Combine first 5 ingredients in medium saucepan. Heat and stir on low for 10 to 12 minutes until margarine is melted.

Brush pineapple quarters with syrup mixture. Preheat electric grill for 5 minutes or gas barbecue to medium (see Note). Cook pineapple on greased grill for about 5 minutes per side, brushing with syrup mixture, until browned. Remove to large serving plate. Cut each pineapple quarter crosswise into 1 1/2 inch (3.8 cm) pieces.

Orange Mascarpone Sauce: Combine all 4 ingredients in small bowl. Makes about 1 cup (250 mL) sauce. Serve with pineapple. Serves 6.

1 serving: 356 Calories; 20.9 g Total Fat (7.9 g Mono, 1.3 g Poly, 10.4 g Sat); 46 mg Cholesterol; 34 g Carbohydrate; 1 g Fibre; 4 g Protein; 194 mg Sodium

Pictured on page 144.

Note: If preferred, arrange pineapple on a greased broiler pan. Broil on the top rack in the oven for about 5 minutes per side, brushing with syrup mixture, until browned.

Potluck Suggestion: Serves up to 12.

Caramel Nut Pudding

Comfort food at its sweet and nutty best. Using dark brown sugar ensures a rich, golden caramel. A winter potluck treat!

All-purpose flour	3/4 cup	175 mL
Chopped pecans, toasted (see Tip, page 22)	1/3 cup	75 mL
Chopped slivered almonds, toasted (see Tip, page 22)	1/3 cup	75 mL
Baking powder	1 1/2 tsp.	7 mL
Salt	1/4 tsp.	1 mL
Can of sweetened condensed milk	11 oz.	300 mL
Milk	2/3 cup	150 mL
Hard margarine (or butter)	2 tbsp.	30 mL
Vanilla	1 tsp.	5 mL
Dark brown sugar (not golden), packed	1 1/4 cups	300 mL
Boiling water	2 cups	500 mL

Combine first 5 ingredients in large bowl. Make a well in centre.

Combine next 4 ingredients in medium saucepan. Heat and stir on medium for about 5 minutes until margarine is melted. Add to well. Stir until just moistened. Spread evenly in greased 2 quart (2 L) casserole.

Sprinkle with brown sugar. Carefully pour boiling water over pudding. Bake in 350°F (175°C) oven for 25 to 30 minutes until just firm. Let stand for 10 minutes. Serves 6.

1 serving: 590 Calories; 18.6 g Total Fat (9.7 g Mono, 2.7 g Poly, 5.3 g Sat); 23 mg Cholesterol; 100 g Carbohydrate; 1 g Fibre; 10 g Protein; 353 mg Sodium

Potluck Suggestion: Serves up to 10.

Dessert Potluck
1. Creamy Peanut Butter Pie, page 129
2. Chocolate Streusel Cake, page 148
3. Peachy Rhubarb Cobbler, page 149
4. Praline Cheesecake Tarts, page 137

Props courtesy of: Casa Bugatti
Cherison Enterprises Inc.
Pyrex® Bakeware

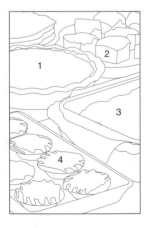

Layered Fruit Salad

Orange cream dresses up fresh fruit for your next potluck.

Block of cream cheese, softened	8 oz.	250 g
Orange juice	1/2 cup	125 mL
Granulated sugar	1/4 cup	60 mL
Chopped fresh mint leaves (or 1 1/2 tsp., 7 mL, dried)	2 tbsp.	30 mL
Grated orange zest	1 tsp.	5 mL
Frozen whipped topping, thawed	2 cups	500 mL
Sliced fresh strawberries	2 cups	500 mL
Fresh blueberries	2 cups	500 mL
Seedless green grapes	2 cups	500 mL
Fresh raspberries	2 cups	500 mL
Fresh mint sprigs, for garnish		

Beat first 5 ingredients in large bowl until smooth. Fold in whipped topping until just combined.

Combine next 3 ingredients in medium bowl. Spoon 1/2 of fruit mixture into large glass serving bowl. Spread 1/2 of cream cheese mixture on top of fruit. Repeat with remaining fruit mixture and cream cheese mixture.

Scatter raspberries over top of cream cheese mixture. Garnish with mint sprigs. Serves 8.

1 serving: 286 Calories; 16.7 g Total Fat (3.5 g Mono, 0.8 g Poly, 11.3 g Sat); 34 mg Cholesterol; 34 g Carbohydrate; 4 g Fibre; 4 g Protein; 101 mg Sodium

Potluck Suggestion: Serves up to 16.

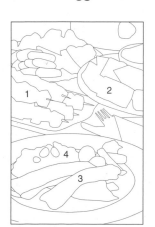

Barbecue Potluck
1. Pork And Apple Skewers, page 84
2. Grilled Pineapple Chunks, page 141
3. Glazed Baby Back Ribs, page 85
4. Sweet Bean Pot, page 112

Props courtesy of: Danesco Inc.
Proctor Silex® Canada

Strawberry Brownie Trifle

A big bowl of tempting trifle, packed full of fabulous flavour.
Impossible to resist—potluck guests will enjoy digging into this!

BROWNIES

Hard margarine (or butter)	1/2 cup	125 mL
Unsweetened chocolate baking squares (1 oz., 28 g, each), chopped	2	2
Brown sugar, packed	1 1/2 cups	375 mL
Large eggs	2	2
Almond flavouring	1 tsp.	5 mL
All-purpose flour	1 cup	250 mL
Chopped walnuts	3/4 cup	175 mL
Almond-flavoured liqueur (such as Amaretto), optional	2 tbsp.	30 mL
Milk	3 cups	750 mL
Boxes of instant vanilla pudding powder (4 serving size, each)	2	2
Sliced fresh strawberries	6 cups	1.5 L
Frozen whipped topping, thawed	2 cups	500 mL
Cocoa, sifted if lumpy (optional)	1/2 tsp.	2 mL
Whole fresh strawberries, halved, for garnish	6	6

Brownies: Heat margarine and chocolate in heavy medium saucepan on lowest heat, stirring often until chocolate is almost melted. Do not overheat. Remove from heat. Stir until smooth.

Add brown sugar, eggs and flavouring. Stir well.

Add flour and walnuts. Stir until just moistened. Spread evenly in greased 9 x 9 inch (22 x 22 cm) pan. Bake in 350°F (175°C) oven for 25 to 30 minutes until wooden pick inserted in centre comes out clean. Remove from oven.

Immediately brush liqueur on brownies. Cool. Cut into 1 inch (2.5 cm) squares. Makes 81 brownies. Set aside.

(continued on next page)

Desserts

Beat milk and pudding powder in medium bowl on low for about 2 minutes until thickened.

Layer ingredients in large glass serving bowl in the following order:

1. 1 cup (250 mL) strawberry slices

2. 1/2 of brownies

3. 1/2 of pudding, spread evenly

4. 2 1/2 cups (625 mL) strawberry slices

5. Remaining brownies

6. Enough of remaining strawberry slices to press against inside edge of bowl to decorate; remainder scattered over brownies

7. Remaining pudding, spread evenly over top

Pipe or dollop whipped topping in decorative pattern on top of pudding.

Sprinkle with cocoa. Garnish with strawberry halves. Serves 16.

1 serving: 295 Calories; 15.5 g Total Fat (6 g Mono, 3.3 g Poly, 5.3 g Sat); 29 mg Cholesterol; 36 g Carbohydrate; 3 g Fibre; 6 g Protein; 293 mg Sodium

Pictured on front cover.

Potluck Suggestion: Serves up to 20.

Paré Pointer

If you want to light up your yard, plant bulbs.

Chocolate Streusel Cake

This moist white cake, crowned with crunchy chocolate nut streusel,
is easy to take to the potluck right in the pan!

Large egg	1	1
All-purpose flour	1 1/2 cups	375 mL
Granulated sugar	3/4 cup	175 mL
Milk	3/4 cup	175 mL
Hard margarine (or butter), softened	6 tbsp.	100 mL
Baking powder	2 tsp.	10 mL
Vanilla	1/2 tsp.	2 mL
Salt	1/2 tsp.	2 mL
STREUSEL TOPPING		
Brown sugar, packed	1/3 cup	75 mL
Hard margarine (or butter), softened	2 tbsp.	30 mL
Chopped walnuts	2 tbsp.	30 mL
Mini semi-sweet chocolate chips	2 tbsp.	30 mL
All-purpose flour	1 1/2 tbsp.	25 mL
Cocoa, sifted if lumpy	1 tbsp.	15 mL
Ground cinnamon	1/2 tsp.	2 mL
White chocolate chips (optional)	1/3 cup	75 mL

Measure first 8 ingredients into large bowl. Beat on low until just moistened. Beat on medium for about 2 minutes until smooth. Spread evenly in greased 9 x 9 inch (22 x 22 cm) pan.

Streusel Topping: Combine first 7 ingredients in medium bowl. Makes about 3/4 cup (175 mL) topping. Sprinkle over batter. Bake in 375°F (190°C) oven for about 30 minutes until wooden pick inserted in centre comes out clean. Let stand in pan on wire rack until completely cooled.

Heat white chocolate chips in small heavy saucepan on lowest heat, stirring often until almost melted. Do not overheat. Remove from heat. Stir until smooth. Drizzle in decorative pattern over cake in pan. Cuts into 9 pieces.

1 piece: 320 Calories; 13.1 g Total Fat (7.5 g Mono, 1.9 g Poly, 3 g Sat); 25 mg Cholesterol; 47 g Carbohydrate; 1 g Fibre; 5 g Protein; 357 mg Sodium

Pictured on page 143.

Potluck Suggestion: Cut into 16 pieces.

Peachy Rhubarb Cobbler

If you like cobbler, you'll find this one just peachy! A light-textured, gently sweet topping crowns a familiar dessert in a brand new way.

Chopped fresh (or frozen, partially thawed) rhubarb	8 cups	2 L
Cans of sliced peaches in light syrup (14 oz., 398 mL, each), with liquid	2	2
Granulated sugar	1 cup	250 mL
Minute tapioca	3 tbsp.	50 mL
WALNUT BRAN TOPPING		
Hard margarine (or butter), softened	1/4 cup	60 mL
Granulated sugar	3/4 cup	175 mL
All-purpose flour	1 1/2 cups	375 mL
All-bran cereal	2/3 cup	150 mL
Chopped walnuts	1/2 cup	125 mL
Baking powder	2 tsp.	10 mL
Salt	1/4 tsp.	1 mL
Milk	1 cup	250 mL

Combine first 4 ingredients in large saucepan. Bring to a boil on medium-high. Reduce heat to medium. Boil gently, uncovered, for about 7 minutes until rhubarb is tender. Spread evenly in greased 3 quart (3 L) shallow baking dish. Keep hot in 400°F (205°C) oven.

Walnut Bran Topping: Cream margarine and sugar in large bowl.

Combine next 5 ingredients in medium bowl. Add 1/2 of cereal mixture to margarine mixture. Stir until mixture resembles coarse crumbs.

Add remaining cereal mixture and milk. Stir until just moistened. Drop mounds of cereal mixture, using about 2 tbsp. (30 mL) for each, on top of hot rhubarb mixture. Bake for about 25 minutes until golden and wooden pick inserted in centre of topping comes out clean. Let stand for 10 minutes. Serves 8.

1 serving: 499 Calories; 11.7 g Total Fat (5.1 g Mono, 3.8 g Poly, 1.8 g Sat); 1 mg Cholesterol; 97 g Carbohydrate; 4 g Fibre; 8 g Protein; 319 mg Sodium

Pictured on page 143.

Potluck Suggestion: Serves up to 16.

Measurement Tables

Throughout this book measurements are given in Conventional and Metric measure. To compensate for differences between the two measurements due to rounding, a full metric measure is not always used. The cup used is the standard 8 fluid ounce. Temperature is given in degrees Fahrenheit and Celsius. Baking pan measurements are in inches and centimetres as well as quarts and litres. An exact metric conversion is given below as well as the working equivalent (Metric Standard Measure).

Spoons

Conventional Measure	Metric Exact Conversion Millilitre (mL)	Metric Standard Measure Millilitre (mL)
1/8 teaspoon (tsp.)	0.6 mL	0.5 mL
1/4 teaspoon (tsp.)	1.2 mL	1 mL
1/2 teaspoon (tsp.)	2.4 mL	2 mL
1 teaspoon (tsp.)	4.7 mL	5 mL
2 teaspoons (tsp.)	9.4 mL	10 mL
1 tablespoon (tbsp.)	14.2 mL	15 mL

Cups

Conventional Measure	Metric Exact Conversion Millilitre (mL)	Metric Standard Measure Millilitre (mL)
1/4 cup (4 tbsp.)	56.8 mL	60 mL
1/3 cup (5 1/3 tbsp.)	75.6 mL	75 mL
1/2 cup (8 tbsp.)	113.7 mL	125 mL
2/3 cup (10 2/3 tbsp.)	151.2 mL	150 mL
3/4 cup (12 tbsp.)	170.5 mL	175 mL
1 cup (16 tbsp.)	227.3 mL	250 mL
4 1/2 cups	1022.9 mL	1000 mL (1 L)

Oven Temperatures

Fahrenheit (°F)	Celsius (°C)
175°	80°
200°	95°
225°	110°
250°	120°
275°	140°
300°	150°
325°	160°
350°	175°
375°	190°
400°	205°
425°	220°
450°	230°
475°	240°
500°	260°

Dry Measurements

Conventional Measure Ounces (oz.)	Metric Exact Conversion Grams (g)	Metric Standard Measure Grams (g)
1 oz.	28.3 g	28 g
2 oz.	56.7 g	57 g
3 oz.	85.0 g	85 g
4 oz.	113.4 g	125 g
5 oz.	141.7 g	140 g
6 oz.	170.1 g	170 g
7 oz.	198.4 g	200 g
8 oz.	226.8 g	250 g
16 oz.	453.6 g	500 g
32 oz.	907.2 g	1000 g (1 kg)

Pans

Conventional Inches	Metric Centimetres
8x8 inch	20x20 cm
9x9 inch	22x22 cm
9x13 inch	22x33 cm
10x15 inch	25x38 cm
11x17 inch	28x43 cm
8x2 inch round	20x5 cm
9x2 inch round	22x5 cm
10x4 1/2 inch tube	25x11 cm
8x4x3 inch loaf	20x10x7.5 cm
9x5x3 inch loaf	22x12.5x7.5 cm

Casseroles

CANADA & BRITAIN		UNITED STATES	
Standard Size Casserole	Exact Metric Measure	Standard Size Casserole	Exact Metric Measure
1 qt. (5 cups)	1.13 L	1 qt. (4 cups)	900 mL
1 1/2 qts. (7 1/2 cups)	1.69 L	1 1/2 qts. (6 cups)	1.35 L
2 qts. (10 cups)	2.25 L	2 qts. (8 cups)	1.8 L
2 1/2 qts. (12 1/2 cups)	2.81 L	2 1/2 qts. (10 cups)	2.25 L
3 qts. (15 cups)	3.38 L	3 qts. (12 cups)	2.7 L
4 qts. (20 cups)	4.5 L	4 qts. (16 cups)	3.6 L
5 qts. (25 cups)	5.63 L	5 qts. (20 cups)	4.5 L

Recipe Index

A

Almond Custard 134
Almond Salad, Orange 91
Almond Shortbread Crust 138
Almond Streusel Topping 136
Appetizers
    California Rolls 12
    Chili Cheese Bean Dip 11
    Crisp Fried Wontons 10
    Eggplant Onion Dip 20
    Ginger Pork Spring Rolls 14
    Layered Tex-Mex Dip 21
    Mini Oriental Spring Rolls 24
    Oriental Wings 16
    Polynesian Meatballs 23
    Surprise Spread 25
    Thai Curry Chicken Wings 22
    Two Bean Dip 19
    Upside-Down Spread 15
Apple Skewers, Pork And 84
Apricot Sauce 23
Arugula Pinwheels, Pepper 123
Asian Dressing 98
Avocado Chicken Buns 121

B

Baby Back Ribs, Glazed 85
Bacon Sour Cream Quiche 49
Bake
    Chicken And Corn 67
    Creamy Hash Brown 103
    Meatball 57
    Rosemary Turkey 62
Baked Zucchini, Cheesy 109
Balsamic Vinaigrette 94
Banana Bread, Chocolate 34
Banana Trifle Squares 140
Barbecue Beef Bunwiches 127
Barbecue Pork, Big Batch 81
Barbecue Sauce 75, 81
Basil Pie, Tomato 56
Bean Dip, Chili Cheese 11
Bean Dip, Two 19
Bean Pot, Sweet 112
Bean-Stuffed Peppers 48
Beef
    Barbecue Beef Bunwiches 127
    Braised Steak Rolls 66
    Cheese And Pasta In A Pot 64

    Chili Beef Stew 74
    Cranberry Meatballs 73
    Ginger Cabbage Rolls 68
    Layered Tex-Mex Dip 21
    Meatball Soup 120
    Pastitsio 58
    Pepper Arugula Pinwheels 123
    Pepper Beef Pinwheels 123
    Polynesian Meatballs 23
    Saucy Meatballs 75
    Swiss Stew 70
Beef And Peanut Salad 96
Big Batch Barbecue Pork 81
Blueberry Bread Pudding 132
Blueberry Sauce 132
Bran Topping, Walnut 149
Bread Pudding, Blueberry 132
Breads & Quick Breads
    Cherry Surprise Muffins 26
    Chocolate Banana Bread 34
    Chocolate-Filled Rolls 31
    Coconut Cranberry Muffins 33
    Flakes Of Oatmeal Bread 38
    Lucky Day Rolls 30
    Oatmeal Buns 39
    Pepper Cornbread Triangles 37
    Poppy Seed Loaf 27
    Pumpkin Pecan Loaf 40
    Pumpkin Pecan Muffins 40
    Sourdough Parmesan Bread 28
    Sourdough Parmesan Buns 29
    Spice-Of-Life Muffins 32
    Zucchini Seed Bread 41
Broccoli And Yam Soup 116
Brownie Trifle, Strawberry 146
Brownies 146
Brunches
    Bacon Sour Cream Quiche 49
    Bean-Stuffed Peppers 48
    Chick And Leek Pie 46
    Creamy Spinach Roulade 44
    Hash Brown Skillet 55
    Pineapple Orange Crêpes 50
    Sesame Seafood Bows 42
    Spinach Feta Pie 52
    Tomato Basil Pie 56
Bumbleberry Streusel Cake 136
Buns
    Avocado Chicken 121
    Chocolate-Filled Rolls 31
    Lucky Day Rolls 30
    Oatmeal 39
    Sourdough Parmesan 29
Bunwiches, Barbecue Beef 127

C

Cabbage Rolls, Ginger 68
Cabbage Salad, Japanese 98
Cakes
    Bumbleberry Streusel 136
    Chocolate Streusel 148
    Pear Flower Gingerbread 133
    Pineapple Upside-Down 128
Cakes, Cheddar Salsa 106
California Rolls 12
Caramel Nut Pudding 142
Carrot Squash Soup, Roast 114
Casseroles
    Cheese And Pasta In A Pot 64
    Chicken And Corn Bake 67
    Layered Veggies And Rice 60
    Meatball Bake 57
    Oriental Rice 63
    Oven-Braised Steak Rolls 66
    Pastitsio 58
    Potato Puff 113
    Rosemary Turkey Bake 62
    Sweet Potato 104
Cheddar Salsa Cakes 106
Cheese And Pasta In A Pot 64
Cheese Bean Dip, Chili 11
Cheesecake, Ginger Pear 138
Cheesecake, Orange Poppy Seed 130
Cheesecake Tarts, Praline 137
Cheesy Baked Zucchini 109
Cheesy Chicken Filling 78
Cherry Icing 26
Cherry Surprise Muffins 26
Chick And Leek Pie 46
Chicken
    Avocado Chicken Buns 121
    Cheesy Chicken Filling 78
    Chick And Leek Pie 46
    Cornmeal Herb 79
    Crisp Fried Wontons 10
    Easy Crispy 77
    Lemon Rosemary 80
    Mini Oriental Spring Rolls 24
    Oriental Chicken Salad 99
    Oriental Rice Casserole 63
    Oriental Wings 16
    Thai Curry Chicken Wings 22
Chicken And Corn Bake 67
Chicken Empanadas 78
Chicken Filling 10
Chicken Sticks 76
Chili Beef Stew 74
Chili Cheese Bean Dip 11
Chocolate Banana Bread 34

Chocolate Crust 134
Chocolate Glaze 31
Chocolate Peanut Crust 129
Chocolate Raspberry Flan 134
Chocolate Streusel Cake 148
Chocolate-Filled Rolls 31
Chowder, New England Clam 117
Chowder, Tex-Mex 118
Chunky Zucchini Soup 119
Clam Chowder, New England 117
Cobbler, Peachy Rhubarb 149
Coconut Cranberry Muffins 33
Coleslaw, Fruity 93
Coleslaw, Thai 95
Company's Coming Classics
    Cheese And Pasta In A Pot 64
    Cranberry Meatballs 73
    Foo Yong Supreme 97
    Japanese Cabbage Salad 98
    Orange Almond Salad 91
    Oriental Wings 16
    Polynesian Meatballs 23
    Surprise Spread 25
    Sweet Potato Casserole 104
    Swiss Stew 70
Corn And Potato Scallop 110
Corn Bake, Chicken And 67
Cornbread Triangles, Pepper 37
Cornmeal Herb Chicken 79
Couscous Salad, Lemony 100
Cranberry Meatballs 73
Cranberry Muffins, Coconut 33
Creamy Hash Brown Bake 103
Creamy Peanut Butter Pie 129
Creamy Pork And Mushrooms 82
Creamy Spinach Roulade 44
Crêpes, Pineapple Orange 50
Crisp Fried Wontons 10
Crispy Chicken, Easy 77
Croissants, Seafood 124
Crusts
    Almond Shortbread 138
    Chocolate 134
    Chocolate Peanut 129
Cucumbers, Marinated 105
Curry Chicken Wings, Thai 22
Curry Marinade 22
Custard, Almond 134

D

Desserts
    Banana Trifle Squares 140
    Blueberry Bread Pudding 132
    Bumbleberry Streusel Cake 136

Caramel Nut Pudding 142
Chocolate Raspberry Flan. 134
Chocolate Streusel Cake. 148
Creamy Peanut Butter Pie 129
Ginger Pear Cheesecake. 138
Grilled Pineapple Chunks 141
Layered Fruit Salad. 145
Orange Poppy Seed Cheesecake 130
Peachy Rhubarb Cobbler 149
Pear Flower Gingerbread 133
Pineapple Upside-Down Cake 128
Praline Cheesecake Tarts 137
Strawberry Brownie Trifle 146
Dilled Potato Salad. 92
Dips
Chili Cheese Bean 11
Eggplant Onion 20
Layered Tex-Mex 21
Two Bean. 19
Dressings, see also Vinaigrettes
Asian 98
Foo Yong 97
Lemon 100
Spicy Peanut 96
Spicy Ranch 99
Sweet Onion 101
Thai 95
Zesty Orange. 93

E

Easy Crispy Chicken 77
Egg Filling 122
Eggplant Onion Dip. 20
Empanadas, Chicken 78

F

Fennel Salad, Peach And 101
Feta Lamb Patties. 88
Feta Pie, Spinach 52
Fillings
Cheesy Chicken 78
Chicken 10
Egg 122
Ginger Pork 14
Guacamole. 121
Oriental Chicken 24
Salmon 122
Shrimp. 124
Fish & Seafood
California Rolls 12
Creamy Spinach Roulade. 44
Japanese Shrimp Salad. 99
New England Clam Chowder. 117

Salmon Loaf Wedges 122
Seafood Croissants. 124
Sesame Seafood Bows 42
Shrimp Filling. 124
Surprise Spread 25
Flakes Of Oatmeal Bread 38
Flan, Chocolate Raspberry 134
Foo Yong Dressing 97
Foo Yong Supreme. 97
Fried Wontons, Crisp 10
Fruit Salad, Layered 145
Fruity Coleslaw. 93

G

Garlic Herb Vinaigrette. 105
Garlic Sauce, Hot 76
Ginger Cabbage Rolls. 68
Ginger Pear Cheesecake. 138
Ginger Pork Filling 14
Ginger Pork Spring Rolls. 14
Gingerbread, Pear Flower. 133
Glaze, Chocolate 31
Glaze, Pepper. 85
Glazed Baby Back Ribs 85
Glazed Roasted Roots. 111
Grilled Pineapple Chunks 141
Guacamole Filling. 121

H

Hash Brown Bake, Creamy 103
Hash Brown Skillet 55
Herb Chicken, Cornmeal 79
Herb Vinaigrette, Garlic 105
Hot Garlic Sauce. 76

I

Icing, Cherry 26
Italian Sausage Risotto 102

J

Japanese Cabbage Salad. 98
Japanese Shrimp Salad 99

L

Lamb Patties, Feta 88
Layered Fruit Salad. 145
Layered Tex-Mex Dip 21
Layered Veggies And Rice. 60
Leek Pie, Chick And 46
Lemon Dressing 100

153

Lemon Rosemary Chicken 80
Lemony Couscous Salad. 100
Loaf, Poppy Seed 27
Loaf, Pumpkin Pecan 40
Loaf Wedges, Salmon. 122
Lucky Day Rolls 30

M

Maple Pear Topping. 138
Marinades
    Curry 22
    Sour Cream 79
    Spicy Orange. 84
Marinated Cucumbers 105
Mascarpone Sauce, Orange 141
Meatball Bake. 57
Meatball Soup 120
Meatballs
    Cranberry. 73
    Polynesian 23
    Saucy 75
Mexican Salad Boats. 99
Mini Oriental Spring Rolls. 24
Muffins
    Cherry Surprise 26
    Coconut Cranberry 33
    Pumpkin Pecan 40
    Spice-Of-Life 32
Mushrooms, Creamy Pork And. 82

N

New England Clam Chowder. 117
Nut Pudding, Caramel 142

O

Oatmeal Bread, Flakes Of 38
Oatmeal Buns. 39
Onion Dip, Eggplant 20
Onion Dressing, Sweet. 101
Orange Almond Salad 91
Orange Crêpes. 50
Orange Dressing, Zesty 93
Orange Marinade, Spicy. 84
Orange Mascarpone Sauce. 141
Orange Poppy Seed Cheesecake 130
Orange Topping. 130
Oriental Chicken Filling 24
Oriental Chicken Salad. 99
Oriental Rice Casserole. 63
Oriental Spring Rolls, Mini 24
Oriental Wings. 16
Oven-Braised Steak Rolls. 66

P

Parmesan Bread, Sourdough 28
Parmesan Buns, Sourdough 29
Pasta
    Cheese And Pasta In A Pot. 64
    Pastitsio 58
    Rosemary Turkey Bake 62
    Sesame Seafood Bows 42
Pastitsio 58
Patties, Feta Lamb 88
Peach And Fennel Salad 101
Peachy Rhubarb Cobbler 149
Peanut Butter Pie, Creamy 129
Peanut Crust, Chocolate. 129
Peanut Dressing, Spicy. 96
Peanut Salad, Beef And 96
Pear Cheesecake, Ginger 138
Pear Flower Gingerbread 133
Pear Topping, Maple 138
Pecan Loaf, Pumpkin 40
Pecan Muffins, Pumpkin. 40
Pecan Salad, Vegetable. 94
Pepper Arugula Pinwheels 123
Pepper Beef Pinwheels 123
Pepper Cornbread Triangles 37
Pepper Glaze 85
Peppers, Bean-Stuffed 48
Pie, Creamy Peanut Butter 129
Pies, Savoury
    Chick And Leek 46
    Spinach Feta 52
    Tomato Basil 56
Pineapple Chunks, Grilled. 141
Pineapple Orange Crêpes. 50
Pineapple Sauce. 50
Pineapple Upside-Down Cake. 128
Pinwheels
    Pepper Arugula 123
    Pepper Beef 123
    Spinach Salami. 123
Polynesian Meatballs 23
Poppy Seed Cheesecake, Orange 130
Poppy Seed Loaf. 27
Pork
    Bacon Sour Cream Quiche. 49
    Bean-Stuffed Peppers. 48
    Big Batch Barbecue 81
    Braised Steak Rolls 66
    Chunky Zucchini Soup. 119
    Creamy Pork And Mushrooms 82
    Foo Yong Supreme. 97
    Ginger Cabbage Rolls 68
    Ginger Pork Spring Rolls 14
    Glazed Baby Back Ribs 85

154

Hash Brown Skillet 55
Italian Sausage Risotto 102
Meatball Bake 57
New England Clam Chowder. 117
Sweet And Sour 86
Sweet Bean Pot 112
Pork And Apple Skewers. 84
Potato Puff Casserole 113
Potato Salad, Dilled 92
Potato Scallop, Corn And 110
Praline 137
Praline Cheesecake Tarts. 137
Pudding, Caramel Nut 142
Pumpkin Pecan Loaf. 40
Pumpkin Pecan Muffins 40

Q

Quiche, Bacon Sour Cream 49
Quick Breads, see Breads & Quick Breads

R

Ranch Dressing, Spicy 99
Raspberry Flan, Chocolate 134
Rhubarb Cobbler, Peachy. 149
Ribs, Glazed Baby Back. 85
Rice
    Bean-Stuffed Peppers 48
    Ginger Cabbage Rolls 68
    Italian Sausage Risotto 102
    Layered Veggies And 60
    Meatball Bake 57
    Meatball Soup 120
    Oriental Rice Casserole. 63
    Sushi 12
Risotto, Italian Sausage. 102
Roast Carrot Squash Soup 114
Roasted Roots, Glazed 111
Rolls, see Buns
Roots, Glazed Roasted 111
Rosemary Chicken, Lemon. 80
Rosemary Turkey Bake 62
Roulade, Creamy Spinach. 44

S

Salads
    Beef And Peanut 96
    Dilled Potato 92
    Foo Yong Supreme. 97
    Fruity Coleslaw. 93
    Japanese Cabbage 98
    Japanese Shrimp 99
    Layered Fruit 145

    Lemony Couscous 100
    Marinated Cucumbers 105
    Mexican Salad Boats 99
    Orange Almond. 91
    Oriental Chicken 99
    Peach And Fennel 101
    Thai Slaw 95
    Vegetable Pecan. 94
Salami Pinwheels, Spinach 123
Salmon Filling. 122
Salmon Loaf Wedges 122
Salsa Cakes, Cheddar 106
Sandwiches
    Avocado Chicken Buns. 121
    Barbecue Beef Bunwiches. 127
    Pepper Arugula Pinwheels 123
    Pepper Beef Pinwheels. 123
    Salmon Loaf Wedges 122
    Seafood Croissants. 124
    Spinach Salami Pinwheels 123
Sauces
    Apricot. 23
    Barbecue 75, 81
    Blueberry 132
    Hot Garlic 76
    Orange Mascarpone 141
    Pineapple. 50
    Tomato 60
Saucy Meatballs 75
Sausage Risotto, Italian. 102
Scallop, Corn And Potato 110
Seafood Croissants 124
Seafood, see Fish & Seafood
Seed Bread, Zucchini 41
Sesame Seafood Bows 42
Sesame Vinaigrette. 42
Shortbread Crust, Almond 138
Shrimp Filling. 124
Shrimp Salad, Japanese 99
Side Dishes
    Cheddar Salsa Cakes 106
    Cheesy Baked Zucchini 109
    Corn And Potato Scallop 110
    Creamy Hash Brown Bake 103
    Glazed Roasted Roots. 111
    Italian Sausage Risotto 102
    Marinated Cucumbers 105
    Potato Puff Casserole 113
    Sweet Bean Pot 112
    Sweet Potato Casserole 104
Skewers, Pork And Apple 84
Skillet, Hash Brown. 55
Soups
    Broccoli And Yam. 116
    Chunky Zucchini 119

155

Meatball. 120
New England Clam Chowder. 117
Roast Carrot Squash. 114
Tex-Mex Chowder 118
West Indies Summer 115
Sour Cream Marinade 79
Sour Cream Quiche, Bacon 49
Sourdough Parmesan Bread 28
Sourdough Parmesan Buns. 29
Spice-Of-Life Muffins 32
Spicy Orange Marinade 84
Spicy Peanut Dressing 96
Spicy Ranch Dressing 99
Spinach Feta Pie. 52
Spinach Roulade, Creamy. 44
Spinach Salami Pinwheels. 123
Spread, Surprise 25
Spread, Upside-Down. 15
Spring Rolls, Ginger Pork 14
Spring Rolls, Mini Oriental 24
Squares, Banana Trifle. 140
Squash Soup, Roast Carrot. 114
Steak Rolls, Oven-Braised 66
Stew, Chili Beef 74
Stew, Swiss. 70
Strawberry Brownie Trifle 146
Streusel Cake, Bumbleberry 136
Streusel Cake, Chocolate 148
Streusel Topping 148
Streusel Topping, Almond 136
Stuffed Peppers, Bean-. 48
Summer Soup, West Indies. 115
Surprise Muffins, Cherry. 26
Surprise Spread 25
Sushi Rice. 12
Sweet And Sour Pork 86
Sweet Bean Pot 112
Sweet Onion Dressing 101
Sweet Potato Casserole 104
Sweet Vinaigrette. 91
Swiss Stew 70

T

Tarts, Praline Cheesecake 137
Tex-Mex Chowder 118
Tex-Mex Dip, Layered 21
Thai Curry Chicken Wings 22
Thai Dressing 95
Thai Slaw 95
Tomato Basil Pie. 56
Tomato Sauce 60
Toppings
    Almond Streusel. 136
    Maple Pear. 138

Orange 130
Streusel 148
Walnut Bran. 149
Trifle Squares, Banana. 140
Trifle, Strawberry Brownie. 146
Turkey Bake, Rosemary. 62
Two Bean Dip. 19

U

Upside-Down Cake, Pineapple 128
Upside-Down Spread 15

V

Vegetable Pecan Salad 94
Veggies And Rice, Layered 60
Vinaigrettes, see also Dressings
    Balsamic. 94
    Garlic Herb. 105
    Sesame 42
    Sweet. 91

W

Walnut Bran Topping 149
West Indies Summer Soup 115
Wings, Oriental 16
Wings, Thai Curry Chicken. 22
Wontons, Crisp Fried 10

Y

Yam Soup, Broccoli And. 116

Z

Zesty Orange Dressing. 93
Zucchini, Cheesy Baked 109
Zucchini Seed Bread. 41
Zucchini Soup, Chunky 119

156

Company's Coming cookbooks are available at retail locations throughout Canada!

EXCLUSIVE mail order offer on next page

Buy any 2 cookbooks—choose a 3rd FREE of equal or lesser value than the lowest price paid.

Original Series — CA$15.99 Canada — US$12.99 USA & International

CODE		CODE		CODE	
SQ	150 Delicious Squares	SF	Stir-Fry	PK	The Pork Book
CA	Casseroles	MAM	Make-Ahead Meals	RL	Recipes For Leftovers
MU	Muffins & More	PB	The Potato Book	EB	The Egg Book
SA	Salads	CCLFC	Low-Fat Cooking	SDPP	School Days Party Pack
AP	Appetizers	CFK	Cook For Kids	HS	Herbs & Spices
SS	Soups & Sandwiches	SCH	Stews, Chilies & Chowders	BEV	The Beverage Book
CO	Cookies	FD	Fondues	SCD	Slow Cooker Dinners
PA	Pasta	CCBE	The Beef Book	WM	30-Minute Weekday Meals
BA	Barbecues	RC	The Rookie Cook	SDL	School Days Lunches
PR	Preserves	RHR	Rush-Hour Recipes	PD	Potluck Dishes NEW *Sept 1/05*
CH	Chicken, Etc.	SW	Sweet Cravings		
KC	Kids Cooking	YRG	Year-Round Grilling		
CT	Cooking For Two	GG	Garden Greens		
SC	Slow Cooker Recipes	CHC	Chinese Cooking		

Lifestyle Series

CODE	CA$17.99 Canada US$15.99 USA & International
DC	Diabetic Cooking

CODE	CA$19.99 Canada US$15.99 USA & International
DDI	Diabetic Dinners
LCR	Low-Carb Recipes
HR	Easy Healthy Recipes

Special Occasion Series

CODE	CA$20.99 Canada US$19.99 USA & International
GFK	Gifts from the Kitchen

CODE	CA$24.99 Canada US$19.99 USA & International
BSS	Baking—Simple to Sensational
CGFK	Christmas Gifts from the Kitchen NEW *Oct 1/05*

Most Loved Recipe Collection

CODE	CA$23.99 Canada US$19.99 USA & International
MLA	Most Loved Appetizers
MLMC	Most Loved Main Courses
MLT	Most Loved Treats
MLBQ	Most Loved Barbecuing
MLCO	Most Loved Cookies NEW *Nov 1/05*

Company's Coming® COOKBOOKS

companyscoming.com
visit our website

Company's Coming Publishing Limited
2311 – 96 Street
Edmonton, Alberta
Canada T6N 1G3
Tel: 780-450-6223
Fax: 780-450-1857
www.companyscoming.com

Order ONLINE for fast delivery!

Log onto **www.companyscoming.com**, browse through our library of cookbooks, gift sets and newest releases and place your order using our fast and secure online order form.

Buy 2, Get 1 FREE!

Buy any 2 cookbooks—choose a **3rd FREE** of equal or lesser value than the lowest price paid.

Title	Code	Quantity	Price	Total
			$	$
DON'T FORGET to indicate your FREE BOOK(S). (see exclusive mail order offer above) please print				

TOTAL BOOKS (including FREE)

TOTAL BOOKS PURCHASED: $

	International	Canada & USA
Plus Shipping & Handling (per destination)	$ 11.98 (first book)	$ 5.98 (first book)
Additional Books (including FREE books)	$ ($4.99 each)	$ ($1.99 each)
Sub-Total	$	$
Canadian residents add G.S.T.(7%)		$
TOTAL AMOUNT ENCLOSED	$	$

Terms

- All orders must be prepaid. Sorry, no C.O.D.'s
- Prices are listed in Canadian Funds for Canadian orders, or US funds for US & International orders.
- Prices are subject to change without prior notice.
- Canadian residents must pay 7% G.S.T. (no provincial tax required)
- No tax is required for orders outside Canada.
- Satisfaction is guaranteed or return within 30 days for a full refund.
- Make cheque or money order payable to: **Company's Coming Publishing Limited.**
- Orders are shipped surface mail. For courier rates, visit our website: **www.companyscoming.com** or contact us: **Tel: 780-450-6223 Fax: 780-450-1857.**

Gift Giving

- Let us help you with your gift giving!
- We will send cookbooks directly to the recipients of your choice if you give us their names and addresses.
- Please specify the titles you wish to send to each person.
- If you would like to include your personal note or card, we will be pleased to enclose it with your gift order.
- Company's Coming Cookbooks make excellent gifts: birthdays, bridal showers, Mother's Day, Father's Day, graduation or any occasion …collect them all!

MasterCard ☐   VISA ☐   Expiry ___ / ___ MO/YR

Account # _____

Name of cardholder _____

Cardholder signature _____

Shipping Address Send the cookbooks listed above to:

☐ **Please check if this is a Gift Order**

Name: _____

Street: _____

City: _____ Prov./State: _____

Postal Code/Zip: _____ Country: _____

Tel: (___) _____

E-mail address: _____

Your privacy is important to us. We will not share your e-mail address or personal information with any outside party.

☐ **YES! Please add me to your newsletter e-mail list.**

Cookmark

Potluck Dishes—Guaranteed Great™ recipes especially created to travel and serve with ease. Find the perfect potluck dish for your next gathering in this collection of all-new recipes, plus 10 Company's Coming Classics. Good food, good friends, good times—potluck!

Quick
&
Easy
Recipes

Everyday
Ingredients

Canada's
**most popular
cookbooks!**

Complete your Original Series Collection!

- ❏ 150 Delicious Squares
- ❏ Casseroles
- ❏ Muffins & More
- ❏ Salads
- ❏ Appetizers
- ❏ Soups & Sandwiches
- ❏ Cookies
- ❏ Pasta
- ❏ Barbecues
- ❏ Preserves
- ❏ Chicken, Etc.
- ❏ Kids Cooking
- ❏ Cooking For Two
- ❏ Slow Cooker Recipes
- ❏ Stir-Fry
- ❏ Make-Ahead Meals
- ❏ The Potato Book
- ❏ Low-Fat Cooking
- ❏ Cook For Kids
- ❏ Stews, Chilies & Chowders
- ❏ Fondues
- ❏ The Beef Book
- ❏ The Rookie Cook
- ❏ Rush-Hour Recipes
- ❏ Sweet Cravings
- ❏ Year-Round Grilling
- ❏ Garden Greens
- ❏ Chinese Cooking
- ❏ The Pork Book
- ❏ Recipes For Leftovers
- ❏ The Egg Book
- ❏ School Days Party Pack
- ❏ Herbs & Spices
- ❏ The Beverage Book
- ❏ Slow Cooker Dinners
- ❏ 30-Minute Weekday Meals
- ❏ School Days Lunches
- ❏ **Potluck Dishes**
  NEW *September 1/05*

COLLECT ALL Company's Coming Series Cookbooks!

Most Loved Recipe Collection
- ❏ Most Loved Appetizers
- ❏ Most Loved Main Courses
- ❏ Most Loved Treats
- ❏ Most Loved Barbecuing
- ❏ **Most Loved Cookies**
  NEW *November 1/05*

Lifestyle Series
- ❏ Diabetic Cooking
- ❏ Diabetic Dinners
- ❏ Low-Carb Recipes
- ❏ Easy Healthy Recipes

Special Occasion Series
- ❏ Gifts from the Kitchen
- ❏ Baking—Simple to Sensational
- ❏ **Christmas Gifts from the Kitchen**
  NEW *October 1/05*

Canada's most popular cookbooks!